A CASE FOR AID

BUILDING A CONSENSUS FOR DEVELOPMENT ASSISTANCE

A CASE
FOR AID

BUILDING A CONSENSUS FOR DEVELOPMENT ASSISTANCE

Includes "A Partnership for
Development and Peace"
by James D. Wolfensohn

THE WORLD BANK
Washington, D.C.

About This Book

A *Case for Aid: Building a Consensus for Development Assistance* is a selection of readings related to the United Nations International Conference on Financing for Development, which was held in Monterrey, Mexico, on March 18–22, 2002.

"A Partnership for Development and Peace" is a keynote speech given by James D. Wolfensohn, president of the World Bank Group, two weeks before the Monterrey event.

"Making the Case for Aid," is a note by Nicholas Stern, World Bank chief economist, discussing the consensus that emerged from Monterrey, including the broad international commitment to reach the Millennium Development Goals by 2015.

"The Role and Effectiveness of Development Assistance" is a report detailing lessons from World Bank experience, which was presented at the Monterrey conference. It was prepared by the Development Economics vice presidency, with input from across the World Bank. The authors are Ian Goldin, Halsey Rogers, and Nicholas Stern.

"The Monterrey Consensus" is the official United Nations document that outlines the major agreements that were reached at the conference. It includes an introduction by Mats Karlsson, World Bank vice president for External and U. N. Affairs.

Contents

Figures

Tables

Part I

A Partnership for Development and Peace

James D. Wolfensohn

President
The World Bank Group

The following is the keynote address given by James D. Wolfensohn, president of the World Bank Group, at the Woodrow Wilson International Center for Scholars, in Washington, D.C., on March 6, 2002. The speech crystallizes the challenges—and opportunities—facing the ministers who attended the United Nations International Conference on Financing for Development in Monterrey, Mexico, in March 2002.

A Partnership for Development and Peace

James D. Wolfensohn

Ladies and gentlemen, I am delighted to be here at the Woodrow Wilson International Center addressing this event cohosted by the Bretton Woods Committee.

Eighty-four years ago in this city, Woodrow Wilson spoke of war and peace to a Joint Session of Congress. "What we demand," he said "is that the world be made safe for every peace-loving nation which, like our own, wishes to live its own life, determine its own institutions, be assured of justice and fair dealing by the other peoples of the world. All peoples are partners in this interest and, for our own part, we see very clearly that, unless justice be done to others, it will not be done to us."

In two weeks in Monterrey, Mexico, leaders from across the world will meet to discuss Financing for Development, when we must all hope that the words of President Wilson will resonate.

Rarely has there been an issue so vital to long-term peace and security, and yet so marginalized in domestic politics in most of the rich world.

Our challenge, as we go forward to the Monterrey Conference and beyond, is to persuade political leaders why that marginalization must end; why justice must be done to others if it is to be done to us; why "all peoples are partners in this interest."

Never perhaps has the chance for concerted action been greater, or the prize more worth the winning. The horrifying events of September 11th have made this a time of reflection on how to make the world a better and safer place. The international community has already acted strongly, by confronting terrorism directly and increasing security. But those actions by themselves are not enough. We will not create that better and safer world with bombs or brigades alone. We will not win the peace until we have the foresight, the courage, and the political will to redefine the war.

3

We must recognize that—while there is social injustice on a global scale, both between states and within them; while the fight against poverty is barely begun in too many parts of the world; while the link between progress in development and progress toward peace is not recognized—we may win a battle against terror, but we will not conclude a war that will yield enduring peace.

Poverty is our greatest long-term challenge. Grueling, mind-numbing poverty—which snatches hope and opportunity away from young hearts and dreams just when they should take flight and soar.

Poverty—which takes the promise of a whole life ahead and stunts it into a struggle for day-to-day survival.

Poverty—which together with its handmaiden, hopelessness, can lead to exclusion, anger, and even conflict.

Poverty—which does not itself necessarily lead to violence, but which can provide a breeding ground for the ideas and actions of those who promote conflict and terror.

On September 11th, the crisis of Afghanistan came to Wall Street, to the Pentagon, and to a field in Pennsylvania. And the imaginary wall that divided the rich world from the poor world came crashing down.

Belief in that wall, and in those separate and separated worlds, has for too long allowed us to view as normal a world where less than 20 percent of the population—the rich countries in which we are today—dominates the world's wealth and resources and takes 80 percent of its dollar income.

Belief in that wall has too long allowed us to view as normal a world where every minute a woman dies in childbirth.

Belief in that wall has allowed us for too long to view the violence, disenfranchisement, and inequality in the world as the problem of poor, weak countries and not our own.

There is no wall. There are not two worlds. There is only one.

The process of globalization and growing interdependence has been at work for millennia.

As my friend Amartya Sen has pointed out, a millennium ago it was ideas—not from the West—but from China, India, and the Moslem world that gave intellectual basis for much of science, for printing, and for the arts. It was the great Mughal Emperor Akbar, a Moslem, who in the 16th century, called for religious tolerance and openness.

There is no wall. We are linked by trade, investment, finance, by travel and communications, by disease, by crime, by migration, by environmental degradation, by drugs, by financial crises, and by terror.

Only our mindsets continue to shore up that wall; we are too set in our ways, too complacent, or too frightened to face reality without it.

It is time to tear down that wall, to recognize that in this unified world poverty is our collective enemy. Poverty is the war we must fight. We must fight it because it is morally and ethically repugnant. We must fight it because it is in the self-interest of the rich to join the struggle. We must fight it because its existence is like a cancer—weakening the whole of the body, not just the parts that are directly affected.

And we need not fight blindly. For we already have a vision of what the road to victory could look like.

Last year, at a summit held at the United Nations, more than 140 world leaders agreed to launch a campaign to attack poverty on a number of fronts. Together, we agreed to support the Millennium Development Goals. By 2015, we said, we will:

- Halve the proportion of people living on less than one dollar a day;

- Ensure that boys and girls alike complete primary schooling;

- Eliminate gender disparity at all levels of education;

- Reduce child mortality by two-thirds;

- Reduce maternal mortality by three-quarters;

- Roll back HIV/AIDS, malaria, and other diseases;

- Halve the proportion of people without access to safe water;

- And develop a global partnership for development.

How could anyone take issue with these goals? How could anyone refuse to stand up and say that for my children and my children's children, I want that better world?

And yet, there are those who legitimately ask: Can we win a war against poverty? And if we can't be sure, should we wager our resources?

To these people I would ask: Can we afford to lose? How much are we prepared to commit to preserve our children's future? What is the price we are willing to pay to make progress in our lifetime toward a better world?

And to the doubters I would say: Look at the facts. For the facts show that despite difficulties and setbacks, we have made important progress in the past, and we will make progress in the future.

- Over the past 40 years, life expectancy at birth in developing countries has increased by 20 years—about as much as was achieved in all of human history prior to the middle of the 20th century.

- Over the past 30 years, illiteracy in the developing world has been cut nearly in half, from 47 percent to 25 percent in adults.

- Over the past 20 years, the absolute number of people living on less than $1 a day, after rising steadily for the last 200 years, has for the first time begun to fall, even as the world's population has grown by 1.6 billion people.

Driving much of this progress has been an acceleration of growth rates in the developing world—more than doubling the income of the average person living in developing countries over the past 35 years.

These are not just meaningless statistics. They indicate real progress in real people's lives:

- In Vietnam, where the number of people in poverty has halved over the last 15 years;

- In China, where the number of rural poor people fell from 250 million to 34 million in two decades of reform;

- In India, where the literacy rate for women rose from 39 percent to 54 percent in just the past decade;

- In Uganda, where the number of children in primary school has doubled;

- In Bangladesh, where dramatic strides have been made to achieve universal primary education—and raised the enrollment of girls in high school to about par with boys, in an environment where girls have faced huge barriers for a long time;

- In Brazil, where the number of AIDS-related deaths have been cut by more than a third;

- Or in Ethiopia, where six million people are now benefiting from better education and health services.

These advances have not come by chance. They have come by action—first and foremost, action by developing countries themselves, but also from action in partnership with the richer world and with the international institutions, with civil society, and the private sector.

But some would say, should we wager our resources on success, knowing that there has also been failure?

Much of the growth and poverty reduction worldwide over the past 20 years have come in the two giants of the developing world, China and India, with progress too in other parts of East Asia and Latin America. Yet, too many countries are being left behind—especially in Sub-Saharan Africa.

There has been too much inequity between countries and within countries, too much exclusion, too many wars, and too much internal strife. And now AIDS threatens to reverse many of the gains made over the last 40 years.

And these challenges will only grow over the next 30 years, as the global population increases by two billion to eight billion people, with almost the entire increase going to developing countries.

As we in the international development community—international institutions and bilateral agencies, governments and NGOs—look to the challenge before us, we must also look objectively back at the past, and do so with humility.

For too many poor people, the Cold War years were years when development stalled or even reversed; when leaders became enriched at the expense of their people; when monies were lent for the sake of politics, not development.

We have seen failure, yes, and we have seen the effects of the politicization of aid; and we must never forget its corrosive impact.

We have learned that policies imposed from London or Washington will not work. Countries must be in charge of their own development. Policies must be locally owned and locally grown.

We have learned that any effort to fight poverty must be comprehensive. There is no magic bullet that alone will slay poverty. But we know too that there are conditions that foster successful development: Education and health programs to build the human capacity of the country; good and clean government; an effective legal and justice system; and a well-organized and supervised financial system.

We have learned that corruption, bad policies, and weak governance will make aid ineffective, and that country-led programs to fight corruption can succeed.

We have learned that debt-reduction for the most highly indebted poor countries is a crucial element in putting countries back on their feet, and that the funds released can be used effectively for poverty programs.

We have learned that we must focus on the conditions for investment and entrepreneurship, particularly for smaller enterprises and farms. But that is not enough for pro-poor growth. We must also promote investment in people, empowering them to make their own choices.

We have learned that development is about the long haul, reaching beyond political cycles or quick fixes—for the surest foundation for long-term change is social consensus for long-term action.

These lessons should give us heart; for more than ever today, bilateral and multilateral donors, governments, and civil society are coming together in support of a set of shared principles.

More than ever today, a new wind is blowing though the world of development, transforming our potential to make development happen.

In this new world, development is not about aid dependence. It is about a chance for developing countries to put in place policies that will enable their economies to grow, that will attract private investment, and that will allow governments to invest in their people—promoting aid independence.

It is about treating the poor not as objects of charity, but as assets on which we can build a better and safer world. It is about scaling up—moving from individual projects to programs. It is about building on and then replicating successes—for example, in community-driven development and microcredit—where the poor are at the center of the solution, not at the end of a handout. It is about forging a New Partnership between rich and poor based on mutual interest and support.

And it is developing countries that are leading the way. Listen to what African leaders are saying in the New Partnership for African Development:

"Across the continent Africans declare that we will no longer allow ourselves to be conditioned by circumstance. We will determine our own destiny and call on the rest of the world to complement our efforts."

These leaders, and leaders and peoples like them through much of the developing world, are recognizing what must be done to allow their countries to develop.

They are committing to good governance, to improving the investment climate, to investing in their people. And the marked improvement in policies in much of the developing world since the 1980s shows that they are serious and are having an effect.

In some countries, these improvements in policies and governance have generated growth, led by the private sector, which involves poor people. By building a more favorable environment for productivity and development, they are creating jobs, encouraging growth in domestic savings and investment, while also spurring increases in foreign direct investment flows.

They are not sitting back waiting for development to be done to them. They are helping to finance their own development; and they recognize the crucial importance of building human capacity within their countries.

But they cannot do it alone.

I have spoken of one side of the new partnership, the leadership in the developing world. But there is also a need for leadership in the developed world, which must grasp the opportunity presented in Monterrey to take the next important step to create that more stable and peaceful world.

What is it that leaders in rich countries should do?

First, they must assist developing countries to build their own capacity in government, in business, and in their communities at large. And in doing so, they must listen to the expressed needs of developing countries so that they help build individual programs that are relevant and can make a real difference. This is not pro-forma work. This is work that requires real commitment and passion.

Second, they must move forward on the issue of trade openness, recognizing that without market access poor countries cannot fulfill their potential no matter how well they improve their policies. The European Union's lead on the Everything But Arms Agreement and the United States's lead on the African Growth and Opportunities Act should be followed by other rich countries now—and the benefits extended to all low-income countries to end the trade barriers that harm the poorest nations and poorest workers. This action does not need to wait on WTO agreement.

There will be powerful political lobbies ranged against any such action. But it is the task of political leaders to remind electorates that lowering of trade barriers will not cost the rich countries anything in the aggregate; they gain from freer trade in these areas, far in excess of any short-term costs of adjustment. There is no sacrifice required, no excuse for failing to take action that would leave all countries better off.

Third, rich nations must also take action to cut agricultural subsidies— subsidies that rob poor countries of markets for their products. Farm support goes mainly to a relatively small number of agribusinesses, many of them large corporations, and yet those subsidies of $300 billion a year are six times what the rich countries provide in foreign aid to a developing world of close to five billion people.

Yes, there are powerful political lobbies ranged against this action too. But the fundamental truth here is that agricultural subsidies constitute a heavy burden on the citizens of developed countries, and a barrier to primary commodity producers in the developing world. With skillful political leadership, they can be cut back. But we need that leadership. And reducing these subsidies would have the additional benefit of yielding significant budgetary savings for governments of rich countries—savings far greater than would be necessary to create very substantial increases in aid together with any internal compensation that may be necessary.

Fourth, rich countries must recognize that even with action on trade or agricultural subsidies, there is still a fundamental need to boost resources for developing countries. We estimate that it will take on the order of an additional $40 to $60 billion a year to reach the Millennium Development Goals—roughly a doubling of current aid flows—to roughly 0.5 percent of GNP, still well below the 0.7 percent target agreed to by global leaders years ago.

Budgetary realities may make it impossible to double aid overnight. But if a New Partnership is to work, we must commit to matching the efforts of developing countries step by step with a phased-in increase in aid—say an additional $10 billion a year for the next five years, building to an extra $50 billion a year in year five.

As part of this support, donors must also conclude an agreement for the funding of the International Development Association (IDA) for the next three years. This program, which provides long-term support for countries with per-capita incomes below $2 a day, is critical for those living in desperate poverty. I believe that an agreement is close on this vital program; the time has come to put it in place. The poor should not be asked to wait.

Does anybody really believe that the goal of halving absolute poverty by 2015 is not worth this investment?

An extra $50 billion in aid would cost only an extra one-fifth of one percent of the income of rich countries.

An extra $50 billion in aid would reverse the decline as a percentage of GDP that has taken place over the last 15 years.

Contrast that with the fact that today the world's leading industrial nations provide nearly 90 percent of the multibillion dollar arms trade— arms that are contributing to the very conflicts that all of us profess to deplore, and that we must spend additional monies to suppress.

Let me repeat:

- We should do it because it is ethically right.

- We should do it because it will make a better, more understanding, more dynamic, and indeed more prosperous world for our children and our children's children.

- We should do it because it will increase the security of all of us, rich and poor.

- We know that disease, the environment, financial crises, and even terror do not recognize national boundaries.

- We know that imaginary walls will not protect us.

If we want to build long-term peace, if we want stability for our economies, if we want growth opportunities in the years ahead, if we want to build that better and safer world, fighting poverty must be part of national and international security. I do not underestimate the challenge of securing an extra $50 billion for development. But I know, as do many others, that this is the place to put our money. The conquest of poverty is indeed the quest for peace.

We must not let our mission be clouded by debates on which there is no disagreement. The debates are: Let's have effectiveness. Let's have productivity. Let's ensure that the money is well spent. Let's ensure that programs and projects are not corrupt. Let's ensure that women are given an important place in the development process. Let's ensure that issues are locally owned. Let's use all instruments at our disposal— grants, loans, and guarantees. These are not issues for debate. They are issues on which the principles are all agreed. These are not issues to hold up action. These are issues on which we can all close ranks and move forward.

Time is not on our side. But perhaps, for once, public opinion is.

There are those that say you will never get support for extra aid in a climate of economic recession and budget cuts. You will never persuade people to look beyond their pocketbooks. I for one do not believe it. I have seen people at their best and at their least selfish in difficult times.

And I believe there is a sea change since September 11th. People everywhere are beginning to recognize:

- that military solutions to terror are not enough,

- that people must be given hope,

- that we must build an inclusive global community, and

- that we must make globalization stand for common humanity, not for commercial brands or competitive advantage.

The understanding is growing. Three months ago a poll of 23,000 people in 25 countries showed overwhelming support for the view that fighting poverty and addressing the gap between rich and poor should top the international agenda.

My friends:

For centuries, we have focused on issues of war and peace. We have built armies and honed strategies. Today we fight a different kind of war in a different kind of world.

A world where violence does not stop at borders; a world where communications sheds welcome light on global inequities; where what happens in one part of the world affects another.

Inclusion, a sense of equity, empowerment, anticorruption—these must be our weapons of the future.

I believe we have a greater chance today than perhaps at any other time in the last 50 years to win that war and forge that new partnership for peace.

Together we must promote understanding that policy can no longer exist in tidy boxes labeled foreign and domestic, home and away— squirreling away 0.1 percent or 0.24 percent of GDP on aid. Together we must persuade finance ministers that when they discuss their budgets, together with defense and domestic spending, they must give equal weight to international spending.

But we must go further. We must change the mindsets that build the walls.

Across the world, we must educate our children to be global citizens with global responsibilities. We must celebrate diversity, not fear it. We must build curricula around understanding, not suspicion; around inclusion, not hate. We must tell our children to dare to be different—international, intercultural, interactive, global.

We must do better with the next generation than we have done with our own.

Let me end, as I began, with the words of Woodrow Wilson—words that reach out across cultural and national divides:

"You are not here merely to make a living. You are here in order to enable the world to live more amply, with greater vision, with a finer spirit of hope and achievement. You are here to enrich the world, and you impoverish yourself if you forget that errand."

Part II

Making the Case for Aid

Nicholas Stern

Chief Economist and Senior Vice President, Development Economics
The World Bank

In this note, Nicholas Stern, chief economist of the World Bank, reports on the main agreements reached at the United Nations International Conference on Financing for Development—held in Monterrey, Mexico, in March 2002—and on the shared understanding of the goals of aid that these agreements reflect. This note also introduces the themes of the World Bank research paper that follows, *The Role and Effectiveness of Development Assistance*.

Making the Case for Aid

Nicholas Stern

There are many cases to be made for development assistance. Different arguments weigh more or less heavily with different people. The paper at the core of this volume, *The Role and Effectiveness of Development Assistance*, focuses on a single question that is central to most arguments for aid: Does aid help to reduce poverty? It finds that, problems and disappointments notwithstanding, aid has generally helped poor countries in their efforts to reduce poverty. Moreover, aid is more effective at reducing poverty today than ever before, due to improvements in poor countries' policies, institutions, and governance (changes that aid has helped to support), and due to better allocation of aid since the end of the Cold War.

Yet merely establishing that aid works does not in itself make the case for aid. It does not, for example, answer the question, Why should rich countries provide aid? Nor does it answer the questions, What are the proper goals of aid? and What do poor countries and rich countries need to do to ensure that aid is as effective as possible? A shared understanding of the answers to these questions has been taking shape in the international community. This understanding, sometimes spoken and sometimes tacit, underpinned the historic global consensus that emerged at the United Nations International Conference for Financing for Development in Monterrey, Mexico, in March 2002. This new approach to these fundamental questions constitutes the case for aid.

Shared understandings made it possible for the leaders of poor countries and rich countries who attended the meeting to promise to work together in a deeper partnership for development. Developing countries declared their determination to continue to strengthen their policies, institutions, and governance, in order to improve their investment climates and invest in their people, thereby providing the framework necessary for rapid, sustained, poverty-reducing growth. Rich countries reaffirmed their willingness to open their markets further to exports from poor countries and to increase financial assistance to poor nations that have shown that they can use it well.

Whether the promises of what has come to be called the Monterrey Consensus are fulfilled will depend in part on the extent to which thoughtful people around the world agree on the answers to these simple but important questions.

Why should rich countries provide aid?

The first question, Why should rich countries provide aid? can be answered in several ways. Here we look at three: an ethical view, a notion of a better world, and an approach based entirely on enlightened self-interest.

A fundamental and crucial ethical argument proceeds from the view that human beings have a basic responsibility to alleviate suffering and to prevent the needless deaths of other human beings. It is a notion that is central to all the major religions of the world. It is a concept of goodness that is founded in the philosophies of classical civilizations. It is part of our understanding of being a decent citizen of the world. To accept the persistence of desperate poverty—that is, to do nothing to change a world where 1.2 billion people subsist on less than a dollar a day, where 120 million children do not attend school, and where tens of millions of people die annually from the combined effects of poor nutrition and diseases that could easily have been prevented or treated—is morally untenable. In such a world, people fortunate enough to be born into the richer societies have a moral obligation to share their good fortune with others.

The ethical motivation for aid is the same motivation that causes a stranger to jump into a river to save a drowning child, heedless of personal danger and without pausing too long to analyze costs, benefits, and risks. Not everyone would choose to help, of course. But most people would recognize that attempting to rescue the child is a response to be admired and welcomed, while not taking action when it could make a difference is morally reprehensible.

The second line of argument mixes elements of altruism with self-interest. It proceeds from the question, What kind of world would I like to live in, and to pass on to my children? Most of us would picture a world in which people behave in a collaborative and supportive manner and where differences are celebrated and valued, as opposed to a world in which people are combative, undermine one another, and are fearful of differences. To create the first kind of world, we must begin by behaving in a manner that brings people together—a manner we would like to see in others. We must work to eliminate widespread deprivation if we want everyone to live in the kind of world we desire for our children. Further, the very act of working together to build a better world helps make this better world a reality.

The third line of argument rests on enlightened self-interest; it is the basest of the three but may nevertheless motivate action. This view recognizes that national borders and geographical barriers that once provided a buffer between rich and poor societies are increasingly porous. Problems of crime, terrorism, illegal drugs, and communicable diseases feed on the hopelessness of extreme deprivation, yet their effects are not confined to poor societies. As James Wolfensohn says in the speech that introduces this book, "there is no wall" separating rich from poor. Like it or not, events and trends in poor and seemingly distant lands can have a direct impact on the lives of people in the rich countries. From this viewpoint, development assistance serves as a sort of preventive maintenance for richer societies. Hence rich countries support poor countries' efforts to reduce poverty in the hope of protecting themselves from the spillover consequences of extreme deprivation.

Managing for Explicit Objectives

In different ways, each of the above justifications for aid assumes that development assistance is, in fact, effective at reducing poverty. Demonstrating this effectiveness depends upon setting explicit objectives toward which progress, in some dimensions at least, can be measured. There also needs to be some agreement on the answers to the second question, What are the proper goals of aid? If we are to work together for development, to manage for explicit objectives, we must define our goals.

The last few years have indeed seen a stronger agreement on the goals of aid. This agreement is best summarized in the Millennium Development Goals (MDGs) adopted at the 2000 United Nations Summit (see box). This set of goals recognizes that poverty is multidimensional: being poor means not only hunger and lack of income, but also ill health and lack of access to education. The goals' ambitious but attainable targets include halving the proportion of people in absolute poverty and cutting child mortality rates by two-thirds over the 25 years ending in 2015. Also by 2015, all children should have the opportunity to attend primary school. The physical environment affects well-being in

---

Millennium Development Goals (1990–2015)

1. Eradicate extreme poverty and hunger
   - Halve the proportion of people with less than one dollar a day.
   - Halve the proportion of people who suffer from hunger.

2. Achieve universal primary education
   - Ensure that boys and girls alike complete primary schooling.

3. Promote gender equality and empower women
   - Eliminate gender disparity at all levels of education.

4. Reduce child mortality
   - Reduce by two-thirds the under-five mortality rate.

5. Improve maternal health
   - Reduce by three-quarters the maternal mortality ratio.

6. Combat HIV/AIDS, malaria and other diseases
   - Reverse the spread of HIV/AIDS.

7. Ensure environmental sustainability
   - Integrate sustainable development into country policies and reverse loss of environmental resources.
   - Halve the proportion of people without access to potable water.
   - Significantly improve the lives of at least 100 million slum dwellers.

8. Develop a global partnership for development
   - Raise official development assistance.
   - Expand market access.
   - Encourage debt sustainability.

---

fundamental ways, so environmental objectives have also been set. The Millennium Development Goals remind us all that, at a time when rich countries are richer than ever, 1.2 billion people still live on less than a dollar a day; we can and must do better.

The goals are interrelated: for example, increases in income help poor people to obtain access to health and education services. Better health and education are important measures of well-being in their own right; they also are often critical means for poor people to improve their lives. Empowering poor people to influence the decisions that shape their lives—through mechanisms such as parental oversight of school management, for example, or beneficiary participation in the design and management of irrigation projects—can speed the attainment of the MDGs.

The fact that poverty is multidimensional does not mean that all aspects of poverty must be attacked everywhere simultaneously and with equal vigor. Priorities will vary across countries and, within countries, across communities. The most effective poverty reduction strategies are locally created and locally owned, and informed by the full range of accumulated international experience.

The different dimensions of poverty captured in the MDGs are only summary statistics and not a simple formula for development. The MDGs do, however, provide a sense of commitment, of urgency, of common purpose. They recognize that poverty has various facets and that there is a common humanity across national and regional boundaries.

The objectives summarized in the MDGs can be related to more fundamental ideas about development and overcoming poverty. These can be summarized in the notions of opportunity, empowerment, and security that were described in the *World Development Report 2000/01: Attacking Poverty*. The report was strongly influenced by *Voices of the Poor*, a study published in three volumes by the World Bank, in which 60,000 people in more than 60 countries were asked to express their own understanding of the meaning of poverty. The multiple dimensions of the MDGs are intermediate objectives that derive from these more basic notions of development and well-being.

How can we work together effectively?

Participants in the Monterrey conference set forth a framework for development cooperation based upon a solid international consensus about what needs to be done; the consensus document is included in this volume. The key components of this framework are three: stronger policies, institutions, and governance in the developing world; trade, including access to the markets of rich nations; and aid.

Commitment by the developing countries themselves is critical to the emerging partnership. A growing number of countries are putting in place the twin pillars of pro-poor growth: the climate for investment, entrepreneurship, and jobs; and the empowerment of and investment in poor people to enable them to participate in the process of development. From the two developing giants, China and India, to smaller countries with circumstances as varied as Bangladesh, Uganda, and Vietnam, developing countries are improving their policies, building institutions, and investing in their people in order to foster rapid, pro-poor growth.

A more open and equitable trading system is the second component of the new development partnership. Such a system moved one step closer to reality in November 2001 when participants in the World Trade Organization (WTO) summit in Doha, Qatar agreed to open a new round of trade talks focused on the needs of developing countries—a "development round." But Doha only opened the door: the hard work is yet to come.

Rich countries can demonstrate their commitment to a new development partnership by opening their markets, individually as well as within the multilateral framework of the WTO. Doing so will not only help poor countries, it will also benefit people in the high-income countries, through lower prices for food and consumer goods, and through lower public expenditures on subsidies. Agricultural subsidies in rich countries are approximately $300 billion a year—similar to the total income in Sub-Saharan Africa and more than five times global net aid flows. Even if narrow self-interest were the only priority for rich countries, these resources could be spent more productively in promoting change within their own borders. Far better, these resources could help poor countries as they boost their spending on health and education, meet the costs of change, and develop the soft and hard infrastructure they need to expand trade and to take part in the world economy. Surely it would be hypocritical of rich countries to ask poor countries to open their markets further without being prepared to make relatively smaller adjustments themselves.

The third element of the partnership framework is aid. As with trade, poor countries are not asking for a handout to consume today but for support in funding the costs of change. There is a clear understanding among developing countries, the international financial institutions, and donors that the opportunity created by enhanced debt relief will not be used to prop up bad policies and sustain poor governance, but to foster change through a greater focus on health and education. Developing countries already finance most of their own development. The target must surely be aid independence.

But to get to aid independence within a reasonable time frame and without unacceptable further hardship to developing countries, rich countries must be prepared to respond on a scale commensurate with the size of the problem. About one-fifth of the developing world subsists on less than $1 per day and nearly half live on less than $2 per day. In the next 30 years there will be about 2 billion more people on the planet, nearly all of them in the developing world. Support must be provided now and in a manner that promotes lasting and sustainable progress. More resources now to fight AIDS, malaria, and tuberculosis can generate enormous returns to health, education, and income growth. Similarly, getting girls into school has a profound effect not only on their own health and income, but also on the health, education, and income-earning ability of their children. Such improvements need not wait for growth to raise incomes: Bangladesh has made dramatic strides towards universal primary education, has raised the enrollment of girls in high school to nearly par with boys, and in the last decade has cut child mortality by half. This has been done first and foremost by internal initiatives, but external support has been fundamental to its success.

Development can work to improve lives. Life expectancy in the developing world has increased by 20 years (from the mid-40s to the mid-60s) over the last four decades—a spectacular achievement when one considers that it must have taken millennia to move from the mid-20s to the mid-40s. The total number of people in absolute poverty has started to fall in the last 20 years, in a sustained way for the first time since the beginning of the 19th century, notwithstanding a rise in population of 1.6 billion over the two decades. But too many countries have been left out. Sub-Saharan Africa, especially, saw no increase in real per capita incomes between 1965 and 1999, even with improved performance in the 1990s. Although Africa did make progress in health and education, the spread of AIDS, along with malaria and tuberculosis, has turned back progress in extending life expectancy.

Fortunately, most developing countries have strengthened their policies, institutions, and governance. Over the last 20 years, developing countries' income per capita has been growing faster than income per capita of the high-income countries, and many poor countries have demonstrated that they can use aid well. In these countries, additional resources can be put to use immediately.

The rich countries have recognized these changes. They also have a deepening sense of the ethical as well as self-interested arguments for aid. Thus during the run-up to Monterrey both the European Union and the United States responded by pledging significant increases in their aid levels over the next few years. The European Union announced plans to raise the average share of GNP devoted to aid to 0.39 percent by 2006; this will be achieved by increasing the level of assistance from countries that fall below the current average of 0.33 percent. Based on current and projected European growth trends, this could imply increasing aid to the equivalent of about $44.7 billion dollars, from the current $25.3 billion dollars. The United States pledged to increase annual aid by $10 billion starting in 2004, an increase of about 50 percent.

Both pledges are important steps in the right direction. They reverse a period of decline in aid, in real terms, during the 1990s. But they are only first steps. James Wolfensohn has suggested that rich countries move gradually but surely to double aid—in line with the improvements in developing country policies already made, and those that will come—by increasing assistance $10 billion each year over the next five years. Coming on top of improvements in the design and allocation of aid since the end of the Cold War, such an increase would provide a significant boost to developing countries' own efforts to reach the MDGs. Indeed, improved policies and governance in developing countries, together with such assistance, could give a real chance of meeting the MDGs for most of the developing world. Even after this doubling of funds, aid would still account for less than 76 cents out of every $100 of rich country government expenditure. Hence it would still be, on average, less than half a percent of rich country income, far lower than the 0.7 percent of GNP that was agreed to internationally decades ago.

As the paper that follows demonstrates, now more than ever aid is a catalyst for change, enabling people to lead longer, healthier, more productive lives. Improvements in the impact of aid have been startling: according to one measure, the number of additional poor people lifted above the $1 per day poverty line by a given quantity of additional aid has increased threefold in the past 10 years. And rich countries have never been richer. The time is right to create a framework for a deep and lasting partnership for development. There is indeed a very powerful case for aid.

Part III

The Role and Effectiveness of Development Assistance
Lessons from World Bank Experience

A Research Paper from the Development Economics Vice Presidency of the World Bank

Ian Goldin, Halsey Rogers, and Nicholas Stern

An earlier version of this paper was presented at the United Nations International Conference Financing for Development held in Monterrey, Mexico, on March 18–22, 2002. It is available online at **http://econ.worldbank.org/.** Comments and questions may be sent to **research@worldbank.org.**

Executive Summary

Foreign aid is increasingly a catalyst for change, and it is helping to create conditions in which poor people are able to raise their incomes and to live longer, healthier, and more productive lives. The past 50 years have seen remarkable successes, as well as failures, in development assistance. Better policies in developing countries, together with improved allocation of aid since the end of the Cold War, imply that aid is more effective today at reducing poverty than ever before.

Yet much of the developing world saw little progress over the past several decades, and in some places, such as parts of Sub-Saharan Africa, living standards declined. Moreover, huge challenges remain, such as reversing the Acquired Immune Deficiency Syndrome (AIDS) and malaria epidemics, and finding ways to spur growth and empower poor people in countries with weak institutions, governance, and policies. An estimated 1.2 billion people subsist on under $1 per day, and the majority of the developing world's population lives on less than $2 per day. (Dollar amounts in this paper are U.S. unless otherwise noted.) Moreover, the world's population will increase by 2 billion in the next 30 years, with almost all of the growth coming in developing countries. How effective the development community is in helping poor societies respond to these challenges will depend on continued learning and on improvements in the allocation, design, and delivery of foreign aid.

This study, *The Role and Effectiveness of Development Assistance: Lessons from World Bank Experience*, takes a broad view of the relationship between development experience and official development assistance (ODA) over the past 50 years, with particular emphasis on the World Bank's experience in recent decades. This report finds that progress in improving well-being has been rapid, if uneven, and that—notwithstanding some significant shortcomings and failures—ODA has often helped to underpin and support success and is becoming more effective in doing so.

The complexity of social and economic change means that the impact of aid cannot be separated easily from other factors. Developing countries themselves bear most of the burdens of development, and rightly claim credit when development succeeds. Assistance works best and can only be sustained when the recipients are strongly committed to development and in charge of the process. In addition, successful projects that draw on foreign assistance in their early stages may later become self-sustaining and serve as models for replication elsewhere, but without any foreign involvement at all. For these and other reasons, the positive impact of ODA can be very large. Nevertheless, identifying cause and effect and attributing outcomes to particular actions is often difficult; furthermore, any excessive attempt to claim credit for the successes of foreign aid can devalue the idea and practice of partnership.

To tackle these analytical problems, this study draws on a variety of types of evidence. We first survey the rapid but uneven progress over the past 50 years and the sources of development success (chapters 1 and 2). Looking more closely at the role of aid, we then consider cross-country statistical analysis (chapter 3) and various types of evidence on the impact of the project, program, and sector lending of the World Bank (chapter 4). We conclude with a discussion of global initiatives. Country examples and insights from country case studies are included throughout the text. Overall, the study presents persuasive evidence that foreign assistance is an increasingly effective tool for reducing poverty and building a more inclusive world. It also recognizes that there are failures as well as successes, and that we can and should learn from both.

Rapid but uneven development progress

In recent decades, development progress has taken place at unprecedented rates in the poorer regions and countries of the world.

- **Health.** Over the past 40 years, life expectancy at birth in developing countries increased by 20 years. It is likely that the previous 20-year increase in longevity took millennia. The improvement resulted partly from higher incomes and better education, particularly of women and girls, but also in large measure from improved knowledge and understanding about the prevention and treatment of disease, and new programs to share this knowledge and put it into practice.

- **Education.** Over the past 30 years, illiteracy in the developing
  world has been cut nearly in half, from 47 percent to 25 percent of
  all adults. Steady expansion of school enrollments worldwide and
  increases in education quality made key contributions to this
  improvement, as did better infrastructure and nutrition.

- **Income poverty.** The number of people subsisting on less than $1
  per day rose steadily for nearly two centuries, but in the past 20
  years it has begun to fall. As a result of better and more market-oriented economic policies through much of the developing world—
  but most importantly in China and India—the number of poor people worldwide has fallen by as much as 200 million, even as the
  world's population has risen by about 1.6 billion since 1980.

*Driving much (though not all) of this progress in income poverty has been an
acceleration in economic growth rates in the developing world.*

- *Since 1965, the per-capita gross domestic product (GDP) of the developing world as a whole has increased by an average of some 2.2 percent per
  year, more than doubling the income of the average developing-country
  resident.* Again, this is a huge change by historical standards and
  substantially higher than growth rates achieved by the developed
  countries in the 19th century and most of the 20th century.

- *Since 1990, developing countries' economies have on average grown
  faster in per capita terms than those of Organisation for Economic Cooperation and Development (OECD) countries (1.9 versus 1.6 percent).*
  This is largely as a result of improved policies, including a stronger
  market orientation, which have created better environments for private-sector growth in many countries.

*This progress on health, education, and income is not accidental.
Governments, with the support of the development community and nongovernmental organizations (NGOs), have accelerated growth and poverty
reduction by improving their policies, institutions, and governance, and
through well-designed projects and programs.*

- *Programs like Progresa in Mexico and the Bolsa Escola in Brazil have
  used financial incentives and parental involvement in school management
  to induce families to keep their children in school,* substantially raising

school enrollments among the poorest children. Progresa, for example, increased secondary enrollment rates by 8 percent for girls and 5 percent for boys in just four years.

- *Targeted action by a global public-private partnership has eliminated the disease of riverblindness from much of West Africa,* following the global community's earlier success in eradicating smallpox from the planet.

- *Bangladesh has cut infant mortality in half (from 140 to 71 per 1,000 live births in the past 30 years), reduced fertility sharply (from 7 births per woman in 1970 to 3.2 births in 1999), and achieved near-universal primary enrollment for girls in an environment where they historically faced high barriers.* The country's innovative NGOs played an especially important role in this progress, but outside assistance was also strongly supportive. While the growth rate of per-capita incomes has not been high in Bangladesh, it has increased in each decade since independence.

- *Market-oriented reforms in Vietnam and China have helped catalyze domestic and foreign investment there,* lifting tens of millions of people out of abject poverty in the former and hundreds of millions in the latter.

These are just a few examples. More systematic evidence presented below and in greater detail in the full paper supports the case that good policies and external support have been the key to progress.

But there have also been major setbacks.

Some regions and countries have grown very slowly or declined in recent decades.

- *Most notably, Sub-Saharan Africa (SSA) as a region saw no increase in its per-capita incomes between 1965 and 1999,* despite some improvement in the 1990s.

- *Although Africa did make steady progress on health and education indicators over much of that period—despite the lack of income growth—the AIDS epidemic has sharply reversed progress on life expectancy in the region.* For the region as a whole, it fell from 50 years in 1990 to 47 years in 1999, and several countries have suffered double-digit declines in life expectancy.

- *Many of the transition economies of Eastern Europe and Central Asia suffered deep declines in living standards and sharp rises in poverty during the 1990s*—although the recession associated with transition has now ended in these countries, and the economies of Central Europe and the Baltics have grown well since the mid-1990s.

The challenge is to extend to all regions and countries the progress that has already improved the well-being of so many people. To do so, the development community must learn from past failures, as well as understand the origins of the successes. Like aid recipients, who have often followed weak policies or allowed institutions to deteriorate, donors also have made mistakes that slowed development.

- *Too often during the Cold War, aid allocations were driven by geopolitical aims rather than by poverty-reduction goals.* Given the diversity of motives, it is not surprising that some of this aid failed to have the direct effect of spurring growth and reducing poverty.

- *Initially, donors placed too much emphasis on the role of what were often isolated projects, neglecting the quality of the overall country environment for growth—a mistake that adjustment (or policy-based) lending was intended to overcome.* Prescriptions for reform were too often formulaic, ignoring the central need for country specificity in the design, sequencing, and implementation of reforms.

- *Adjustment lending had its own problems. Donors incorrectly believed that conditionality on loans could substitute for country ownership of reforms.* Too often, governments receiving aid were not truly committed to reforms. Moreover, neither donors nor governments focused sufficiently on poverty in designing adjustment programs.

- *In many countries, donors underestimated the importance of governance and institutional reforms and of social investments as a complement to macroeconomic and trade reforms.* As a result, weak governance and institutions reduced the amount of productivity growth and poverty reduction that could result from the macroeconomic reforms.

- *Many of these factors came together in Africa, contributing to the lack of progress in the region.* There are many causes to slow development in Africa, including poor domestic policies and institutions and weak commitment to reform, but too often aid did little to improve the situation and in some cases even worsened it.

From these cases and others, donors have drawn lessons, and are now showing greater selectivity in lending, shifting resources toward governance and institutions, emphasizing ownership, and making room for diverse responses to local needs. These new approaches and procedures have begun to pay off. However, it is clear that there is still much to learn: for example, on the question of how best to catalyze and support reforms and institution-building in countries with very weak policies, institutions, and governance.

Understanding the sources of development outcomes

The development community has been learning about what development means and how to achieve it.

The understanding of development has evolved. It is now widely accepted that poverty reduction efforts should address poverty in all its dimensions—not only lack of income, but also the lack of health and education, vulnerability to shocks, and the lack of control over their lives that poor people suffer. This understanding of poverty in some cases implies different approaches than in the past—for example, an increased focus on public service delivery to vulnerable groups, as well as greater attention to early disclosure of information that poor people can use. This multidimensionality of poverty is embodied in the Millennium Development Goals (MDGs) adopted by heads of state at a United Nations summit in 2000.

Knowledge about what works and what does not work has also improved. Experience has shown that neither the central planning approach followed by many countries in the 1950s and 1960s, nor the minimal-government free-market approach advocated by many people in the 1980s and early 1990s, will achieve these goals. Most effective approaches to development will be led by the private sector, but with effective government to provide the governance framework, facilitation or provision of physical infrastructure, human capital investments, and social cohesion necessary for growth and poverty reduction. Institutional development has too often been neglected in past policy discussions, but is now recognized to be essential to sustained poverty reduction.

While a number of key principles for effective development are clear, there is no single road to follow. Countries must devise their own strategies and approaches, appropriate for their own country circumstances and goals.

We have improved our understanding of the main sources of growth and poverty reduction, although there is still much to learn. Two pillars of development are essential: an investment climate that encourages private-sector productivity growth and job creation, and mechanisms to invest in and empower poor people so that they can participate in growth.

Promoting development requires spurring the growth of private investment and productivity. Development assistance will never be able to achieve desired outcomes on its own, no matter how well designed and implemented the projects, simply because levels of development assistance are small relative to other financial flows and to the scale of the challenge at hand. Development aid totaled about $54 billion in 2000; this was only one-third as much as foreign direct investment in developing countries ($167 billion), which itself was only a small fraction of total investment (nearly $1.5 trillion). This underscores the point that when aid makes a major difference in the fight against poverty, it does so through demonstration effects or improvements in institutions, not simply through resource transfer. To meet the challenge of "scaling up," aid must help countries put in place for themselves the pillars of development that will support rapid and shared private-sector-led growth.

Experience and analysis show that countries reduce poverty fastest when they put in place two pillars of development:

- **Create a good investment climate**—one that encourages firms and farms, both small and large, to invest, create jobs, and increase productivity.

- **Empower and invest in poor people**—by giving them access to health, education, infrastructure, financial services, social protection, and mechanisms for participating in the decisions that shape their lives.

Understanding of economic growth and its causes has improved. We now understand that creating an investment climate that sustains growth requires progress in a number of areas: macroeconomic stability and trade openness; governance and institutions (including a good education system, an effective legal and judicial system, a professional bureaucracy, a strong and well-regulated financial sector, and vigorous competition); and adequate infrastructure.

This improved understanding does not mean that all growth challenges have been solved. One major issue is the appropriate sequencing and selection of policy and institutional reforms. No poor country has the capacity to move forward with equal vigor on all these fronts at once, so it will be important for the country, with external support, to focus on identifying and grappling with the main obstacles to growth. A second challenge is consistency: many countries manage to achieve growth spurts of several years, but find it very difficult to achieve the two or three decades of consistent growth necessary for sustained poverty reduction.

Poverty reduction depends heavily on sustained economic growth. On average across countries, income distribution does not worsen during periods of economic growth, so that on average the incomes of poor people rise at a similar rate to those of wealthier people. Countries that grew rapidly in the 1990s—such as China, India, Vietnam, and Uganda—managed to reduce the share of their people in absolute poverty by 5 to 8 percent per year.

While growth is essential, it is also important to recognize that these are just averages, and that there is a good deal of variation across countries, regions, and groups. Countries can accelerate their reduction of income poverty by acting to ensure that poor people have the tools necessary to participate in growth; in other words, they can promote pro-poor growth. Of special importance here are health and education, as they also have a direct impact by reducing poverty in key non-income dimensions. In these and other areas, promoting gender equality yields major development benefits: healthy and educated women are more productive, have healthier and better educated children, and even contribute to improved governance. Other services that equip poor people to participate include infrastructure and financial services, which often fail to reach them. Furthermore, participation of poor people in the decisions that most affect their lives—for example, parental involvement in school management or participation by beneficiaries in project design—is a key part of fostering the involvement of poor people in the growth process.

Policies and investments aimed directly at reducing nonincome dimensions of poverty can be highly effective. Countries can accelerate health and education progress far beyond what would result simply from economic growth. Without targeted measures, economic growth only slowly improves health and education. On the other hand, progress in these dimensions can serve as a major stimulus to growth.

Globally, we see the powerful effects of policy in the dramatic reductions in infant mortality, which has fallen steadily at each level of income as a result of improvements in technology, knowledge, and policies and institutions. For example, the average country with $8,000 per capita income in 1950 (measured in 1995 dollars) would have had an infant mortality rate of 45 per 1,000 live births; by 1995, an average country at the same income level would have had an infant mortality rate of just 15 per 1,000 live births, a reduction of two-thirds.

Many developing countries have acted on advances in understanding and knowledge by improving policies and institutions, often with strong results.

The development progress that we have seen in many countries can be attributed primarily to actions by the countries themselves: specifically, improving the investment climate and investing in people.

Macroeconomic stability and openness have improved throughout the developing world over the past two decades. The median inflation rate of developing countries was cut in half between 1982 and 1997, from about 15 to 7 percent. Average tariff rates have also declined sharply in all developing regions. In South Asia, for example, the unweighted average tariff fell from about 65 percent in 1980–85 to about 30 percent in 1996–98; and in Latin America and the Caribbean, from about 30 percent to under 15 percent in 1996–98.

A group of countries that has integrated most quickly with the global economy—thanks to greater openness and improved investment climates—has grown very rapidly. This group that showed the strongest advances in trade integration, accounting for some 3 billion of the developing world's 5 billion people, saw per-capita incomes increase by a remarkable 5 percent per year in the 1990s. Even with fast-growing China excluded, the average was 3.5 percent. By comparison, per-capita growth in the high-income economies was only 2 percent. Integration, it should be stressed, is not about applying a simplistic liberalization formula. Both China and India are part of this group because of their rapid trade growth and strong movement toward more-open markets, even though their economies are not among the most open in the developing world in terms of import liberalization.

Complementary actions by rich countries are essential. One key area is in trade policy. Trade protection in the rich countries, particularly in agriculture and textiles, blocks the exports and undermines the competitiveness of many countries. Poor countries bear the brunt of this protection, as they face tariffs twice as high on average as those applied to the products of rich countries. Protection greatly reduces the growth rewards of reform in poor countries.

Yet too many countries have lagged and some have declined.

The economic decline in much of Sub-Saharan Africa stems in part from events beyond African countries' control, including large and persistent declines in the prices of commodities that they export and high country-risk perceptions that deter investment. But many African countries compounded the external problems by failing to promote good policies and institutions. Although policies have improved sharply in recent years, governance and institutions remain a major challenge in most of these countries.

Countries that have not grown rapidly—in Africa and elsewhere—have often failed to make progress on key features of the investment climate. For example, they may have achieved macroeconomic stability but not social stability; or they may have lowered trade barriers but not built the basic infrastructure necessary for international trade; and some have done none of these things. As we have learned from experience, macro-economic stabilization and liberalization are important steps, but they are not generally enough by themselves to promote lasting development.

Nevertheless, there are countries in which the rewards of reform have been far less than predicted. These countries have made many of the reforms advocated by external parties but have either seen little growth response or have not seen growth translate into rapid poverty reduc-tion. In some cases, geographic challenges have hindered growth; in other cases, a history of poor policies has led investors to doubt the per-manence of recent improvements. In such cases, the development com-munity should work to help sustain these reforms and increase their returns.

The role of development assistance:
Country examples and cross-country evidence

This paper aims to assess how development assistance has contributed to the development progress of recent decades. Development assistance encompasses both financial and nonfinancial instruments that are aimed at supporting the recipient country's efforts to accelerate growth and reduce poverty.

Resource transfer is an important part of development assistance, and the quantitative analysis in this section will focus largely on assessing its effects. But finance is only one of the instruments used to support development and, in some situations, it is not even the most useful one. Development assistance also includes analysis, advice, and capacity-building. Many of the country boxes in this paper highlight the importance of these nonlending tools, especially in situations—such as early in a reform era—when finance is not likely to contribute to poverty reduction. The mixture of instruments to be used in any particular country depends on the specifics of that country's needs and capacity.

Attempts to assess the contributions of external assistance face inherent difficulties. Dealing with them requires the use of a variety of types of evidence.

The most successful development assistance will have effects that reverberate far beyond the confines of the project itself, either because the ideas in the project are replicated elsewhere, or because the intervention has helped institutionalize new approaches. As noted above, levels of aid are small relative to the private capital and public resources that it can leverage, so that aid's largest impacts will come through such demonstration effects and institution-building. But these wider or deeper effects of aid will be far harder to measure than its direct effects.

Furthermore, successful development strategies and actions generally depend on strong country ownership, as well as good partnership among donors; both make it difficult, and even counterproductive, for any external actor to claim full credit for a reform or project. For these reasons, this paper makes use of several types of evidence—cross-country statistical analysis, program and project evaluations, case studies, and analyses of global programs—in trying to assess the role and effectiveness of development assistance.

Because each country is unique, the role of aid can be understood best through careful analysis of individual countries. In the body of this paper, detailed country examples are included in each section. In the interests of brevity, this executive summary presents some snapshots of aid in action at the country level before proceeding to the cross-country statistical analysis.

Uganda, Mozambique, China, Vietnam, India, and Poland are all examples of countries where, within the past two decades, policy and institutional reforms have sparked an acceleration in development. In each of these cases, the country and its government have been the prime movers for reform, and each country mapped out its own development strategy and approach. Their experiences do have some common features—most notably an increase in market orientation and macroeconomic stability—and all have seen their growth powered by private sectors (both farms and firms) that have begun to thrive. But while these countries did act along those broad guidelines on development, none of them closely followed any external blueprint for development offered by the Bank or other donors.

Yet in all of these cases, development assistance from many sources has supported the transformation. In some cases, advice was more important than lending. In the case of China, for example, aid flows have been dwarfed by inflows of private capital. But development assistance helped pave the way for private-sector growth and international integration—for example, when the World Bank and others provided analysis and advice to help China open its economy to investment, unify its exchange rate, and improve its ports early in the transition period. And advice without commitment of resources and people is less likely to be taken seriously.

The examples here focus mainly on contributions made by the Bank—again, in support of country-owned and country-implemented reforms—but other donors have also been influential.

- **China.** The past 20 years of reform in China have contributed more to poverty reduction than any other growth episode in history. Unquestionably, this process of growth and development was driven by China itself. The composition, sequencing, and timing of reforms were designed at home, and built on China's existing strengths in such areas as literacy and basic health. At the same time, support from outside helped make reform happen and contributed to the structure of the reforms. In the early stages of market-oriented reform, the World Bank provided advice on laying the foundation for the private investment and productivity growth that has buoyed the country's remarkable progress. The Bank provided the government with the first in-depth overall analysis of China's economic problems, and it helped China engage with the outside world (again, on the country's own schedule) through advice on liberalization, exchange-rate unification, and port modernization. The Bank's rural development projects and analytical work complemented strongly these improvements in the overall business environment by targeting poverty where it was most prevalent—in the countryside. The Bank, as both a knowledge and lending institution, thereby made a significant supporting contribution to the massive reduction in rural poverty: from 34 percent of the rural population in 1985 to just 18 percent in 1998.

- *India.* Throughout the 1960s and 1970s India was weakly integrated into the international economy and relied heavily on planning and licensing; as a result, economic growth and poverty reduction were unimpressive. Growth accelerated in the 1980s but was based in large measure on unsustainable public spending and foreign borrowing. With the entry of a reformist government in 1991, the Bank provided support for trade and other reforms to stabilize and open up the economy. Over the past five years, the Bank has supported India's decentralization process, working closely with state, local, and municipal governments committed to reform. Powerful demonstration effects are beginning to emerge.

- *Mozambique.* Mozambique is a recent example of successful post-conflict reform. The country emerged in 1992 from a long civil war, which—combined with a socialist experiment—had left the country one of the poorest in the world. Since then the World Bank has helped the government to design and implement exchange rate reform, trade liberalization, financial liberalization, and privatization. In this more stable and open environment, GDP has grown at an average rate of 8.4 percent—in part due to revitalized agricultural growth and to increasing exports, which had been stagnant for a decade. The private sector has responded: foreign direct investment (FDI) grew some 500 percent between 1992 and 2001. Today, the focus has shifted towards two areas of continued weakness: strengthening the social sectors (Mozambique is struggling against the AIDS epidemic), and reforming judicial and tax systems.

- *Uganda.* Uganda's new government in the mid-1980s inherited a country that was devastated by years of conflict and economic mismanagement. Starting with advice, the Bank helped the government learn from the comparative experience of Ghana and other countries and helped it design and implement key measures on fiscal adjustment, exchange rate reform, and trade liberalization. Aid and the conditionality associated with Bank-supported adjustment lending helped generate policy reforms in the late 1980s and early 1990s, a period during which multilateral assistance from the Bank and other lenders was particularly important. Since that period, Uganda has achieved a remarkable recovery: it has increased private investment, reversed capital flight, increased external trade, and privatized commercial public enterprises. It has made great strides in primary education, with several million additional children attending school during the first year of a Bank adjustment loan. Uganda has also reversed income poverty sharply, from 56 percent in 1992–93 to 35 percent by the year 2000.

- **Poland.** Poland was the first country to emerge from the transition recession in 1992 and has since maintained an average GDP growth rate of 3.7 percent, the highest among transition economies. Positioned to gain access to the European Union (EU) in 2004, Poland has led the way in many reforms, often taking major risks. Outside assistance has also helped. From the early phases of Poland's economic transformation, the Bank provided advisory and financial support. Activities included aiding macroeconomic reforms, supporting the creation of an institutional and regulatory framework, helping with the restructuring and privatization of industries, upgrading infrastructure with private-sector participation, and helping to restore Poland's creditworthiness. Finally, the Bank also helped to improve public understanding of the government's economic strategy.

- **Vietnam.** Vietnam has also moved strongly to reform its economy and reduce poverty over the past dozen years, beginning when it was still politically and economically estranged from major donors and therefore could not receive large-scale aid. The Bank began to provide advice to Vietnam in 1989, at a time when the country's disastrous economic policies had produced a crisis of hyperinflation, falling economic activity, and mass exodus of economic migrants. Although it did not provide finance until 1993, the Bank advised the government on stabilizing the macroeconomy, opening to foreign trade and investment, and reforming property rights. As reforms took hold, the Bank later shifted its focus to infrastructure and primary education. The results have been remarkable: the income poverty rate was cut from 58 to 37 percent in just six years.

These six countries provide recent examples of Bank-supported progress, but the past 50 years of development experience also provide examples—such as the Republic of Korea and Botswana—that illustrate how effective aid can be in supporting reform. Korea, for example, progressed from borrowing from the International Development Association (IDA), the Bank's soft-loan facility for the poorest countries, to borrowing from the International Bank for Reconstruction and Development (IBRD), the lending arm for middle-income countries, and finally to borrowing solely in private markets. Korea is also an example of a country that, with donor support, built both pillars of development: it invested heavily in education and human development while also greatly improving the environment for growth and entrepreneurship.

It is important to note that impressive development results do not depend on reaching all goals simultaneously. Each of the countries listed here continues to face major development challenges, whether in governance or institution-building or capacity development. However, these examples show just how strong the returns can be to moving in the right direction, and how important it is to help countries that are committed to making this movement.

Of course, the World Bank has also been involved in many countries, particularly in Sub-Saharan Africa, where results have been less impressive. There are too many countries that have received very large volumes of aid over time, with little result in terms of poverty reduction. For example, between 1960 and 2000, donors disbursed more than $10 billion in aid to the Democratic Republic of Congo (formerly Zaire)—a country that, for most of that period, showed little inclination to take the steps necessary for development. Indeed, GNP per capita fell strikingly for much of that period, from $460 in 1975 to $100 in 1996. And as noted above, donor-supported progress on human development indicators has been reversed by the AIDS epidemic or by conflict in many African countries. In Botswana, which otherwise has a highly successful economy, AIDS reduced life expectancy from 57 years to 39 years in the 1990s; in Sierra Leone, conflict and chaos have kept life expectancy at around 35 years. The Bank and other donors provided substantial support for governments that were not willing to take decisive action against AIDS, and other development failures have helped provide a fertile ground for civil conflict.

Cross-country statistical evidence confirms that the positive role of assistance extends well beyond these country-specific examples. Development assistance has, in general, accelerated growth and poverty reduction, and its poverty-reduction impact has increased over time.

The statistical evidence shows that large-scale financial aid can generally be used effectively for poverty reduction, where reasonably good policies are in place. The World Bank and other donors have acted on these findings by tailoring support to local needs and circumstances. Thus the balance of support has moved toward providing large-scale aid to those that can use it well and focusing on knowledge and capacity-building support in other countries.

By this criterion, donor financial assistance is targeted far more effectively at poverty reduction than it was a decade ago. At that time, Cold War geopolitics was still exercising a heavy influence on aid allocations, and too many recipient economies were poorly run, often suffering from excessive state intervention in economic activity and poor governance.

- In 1990, countries with worse policies and institutions—as assessed by Bank diagnostics—received $44 per capita in ODA from all sources (multilateral and bilateral), while those with better policies received less: only $39 per capita.

- By the late 1990s, the situation was reversed: better-policy countries received $28 per capita, or almost twice as much as the worse-policy countries ($16 per capita).

As a result, the poverty-reduction effectiveness per dollar of overall ODA has grown rapidly.

- In 1990, a one-time aid increase of $1 billion allocated across countries in proportion to existing ODA would have permanently lifted an estimated 105,000 people out of poverty; but by 1997–98, that number had improved to 284,000 people lifted out of poverty. (Poverty is defined here as living on less than $1 per person per day, adjusted for cross-country differences in living costs.) *In other words, the estimated poverty-reduction productivity of ODA nearly tripled during the 1990s.* And it must be emphasized that movements of people above the poverty line represents just one impact of the aid, which also helped increase income and other dimensions of development throughout the economy.

Yet despite the improvement in aid effectiveness, donor countries did not respond with an increase in aid flows; instead, aid levels fell.

- Aid flows dropped substantially over the 1990s in real terms, and by 2001 were 20 percent below the 1990 level in inflation-adjusted terms.

- With the growth in incomes in the rich countries over the 1990s, aid levels expressed as a share of donors' GNP fell even more sharply—from 0.33 percent in 1990 to 0.22 percent in 2000.

World Bank assistance is relatively efficient at reducing poverty.

IDA funds are relatively well focused on poor countries that have shown they can use aid effectively.

- As with ODA in general, too often in the past IDA allocations have been driven by considerations other than poverty reduction. And even where poverty has been the focus, the Bank has often been overly optimistic about the prospects for reform, thereby contributing to misallocation of aid.

- Nevertheless, even in 1990, much more IDA funding went to the good-policy countries ($4.7 per capita) than to the poor-policy countries ($2.0 per capita). By the late 1990s, targeting had improved still further: good-policy countries now receive $6.5 per capita, compared with $2.3 per capita in poor-policy countries.

As a result, an additional $1 billion allocated in the same way as existing IDA funds in 1997–98 would, by this measure, have lifted an additional 434,000 people permanently out of poverty. This means that IDA is not only 60 percent more efficient than it was in 1990, but also 50 percent more efficient than overall ODA. Again, the effect on numbers crossing the $1 per day poverty line is just one effect of additional IDA funding. IBRD (nonconcessional) lending also goes primarily to countries with good policies and institutions.

Well-targeted aid (such as IDA funding) helps to attract private investment by improving the investment climate. As a result, it has very high overall returns.

- *Much IDA lending is targeted at improving the investment climate, by supporting improved policies and building the governance,*

institutions, and infrastructure necessary for private-sector productivity.

- As a result, every dollar of IDA funding on average leads to an
  increase in gross investment of nearly two dollars. In good policy
  environments, aid also increases foreign direct investment substantially—by 60 cents for each dollar of aid.

- This "crowding-in" effect means that the returns to IDA funding far
  exceed the poverty-reduction returns. It is estimated that the overall
  return—in terms of the income growth spurred by IDA—may be as
  high as 40 percent.

*Well-designed adjustment lending to countries committed to reform is general-
ly effective in accelerating poverty reduction, in part as a result of lessons
learned during the early difficulties with adjustment in the 1980s and early
1990s.*

Adjustment lending was developed as a necessary corrective, after distorted macroeconomic environments had been shown to undermine
the effectiveness of project-level assistance. Early experience with
adjustment lending was uneven and revealed problems: lending was
not sufficiently selective, with too much money going to countries
with poor reform and implementation records, and the design and
implementation paid insufficient attention to social costs, institutions,
and the dynamics of reform. Since then, adjustment lending has
improved in targeting and design. It is now generally an effective way
of providing strong reform support in countries with adequate policy
and institutional frameworks. By the 1990s, adjustment lending was
earning higher internal Bank evaluation ratings (as judged by the independent Operations Evaluation Department) than investment lending.
And attention to the distributive impact of reforms has improved,
although further learning is still necessary.

*One broad lesson from experience is that reform does not usually succeed
without strong local ownership; this lesson has provided the impetus for the
Poverty Reduction Strategy Paper (PRSP) process.*

At the society-wide level, early evidence suggests that the PRSP
process is increasing both ownership (through participatory discussion

of reform alternatives) and poverty focus of development programs in low-income countries. Although it is too early to gauge outcomes on the ground, full PRSPs are so far associated with a 20-percent increase in spending in poverty-related areas. A similar shift in the balance of spending is associated with the Highly Indebted Poor Country (HIPC) debt relief programs developed since the mid-1990s and led by the World Bank and International Monetary Fund (IMF).

World Bank effectiveness at the program/sector/project level

Measured results show that the Bank's actions have been broadly successful in promoting higher productivity and human development, especially over the past decade.

Bank operations have served in general to increase the economic productivity of borrowers. The minimum economic rate of return (ERR) expected from Bank-financed projects is 10 percent. Although there is considerable variation, and there have been failures, actual results have been substantially better, reaching an average of 16 percent in the 1980s and rising to 25 percent in the 1990s. Bank operations also make a difference in the areas of health and education.

The Bank is the world's largest external funder of education, having provided a cumulative $30 billion for education projects. It also is the world's largest external funder of health programs, with new commitments of $1.3 billion a year for health, nutrition, and population projects. These projects had significant results in themselves and were often replicated outside of the original project area. Although it is not possible to quantify this overall effect, country experiences are indicative. In China, for example, a project in the late 1990s helped raise the proportion of households using iodized salt from 40 to 89 percent, reducing iodine deficiency in targeted age groups from 13 to 3 percent. Ultimately, this will result in average gains of 10 to 15 points in children's IQ levels in affected communities. In Mali, a project in the early 1990s raised the share of children fully vaccinated from 0 to 24 percent. In the education sector, girls' enrollment in Bangladesh has increased dramatically — from 34 percent of secondary-school enrollment in 1990 to 48 percent in 1997 — with support from a Bank project. And beyond these direct effects, economic growth supported by the Bank often indirectly improves social indicators, although countries need to strengthen this link by prioritizing health and education for poor people.

Bank lending generally encourages good economic performance. Reviews of adjustment lending show that in the 1990s, it supported governments in maintaining their efforts in social areas and in poverty focus. Developing countries receiving Bank adjustment lending in 1990–97 maintained and even increased social expenditures, on average, more frequently than countries without such lending.

The outcomes of Bank lending have improved steadily. Project outcomes have improved sharply over the past decade. Despite the growing complexity and more demanding nature of its development agenda, the Bank has increased its share of projects rated as satisfactory from well below 60 percent in the late 1980s to above 80 percent today.

The Bank has increased its effectiveness by incorporating lessons from experience.

These improvements in outcomes come as a result of attempts to learn from experience and adapt to changing circumstances. In part due to increases in private capital flows and changing government priorities, as well as due to changing understanding of the Bank's role, the Bank has shifted the sectoral composition of its lending. It has shifted resources away from direct infrastructure lending (which fell from three-quarters of Bank lending in the 1960s to one-third in the 1990s) and toward the social sectors (now one-fifth of the total). This shift has been made possible in part by the increased role of the private sector in some areas of infrastructure; in those areas, the Bank now focuses its efforts on facilitating the environment for improvements in infrastructure, including through regulatory reform.

The Bank has also increased both the quantity and quality of policy-based lending. As a result of greater selectivity, adjustment operations achieved their objectives in more than 80 percent of cases in the 1990s—up from 60 percent in the 1980s—and the share with a poverty focus rose sharply. The same shift towards social spending has occurred in the programs associated with debt relief for HIPC; indeed, this is a principal goal of these programs.

Other improvements include:

- **Stronger quality management,** by identifying key features of successful projects and applying quality controls at earlier stages of design and implementation;

- **Sharper country focus.** Bank assistance is provided through the framework of country assistance strategies. These are now developed in consultation with governments, and increasingly with NGOs, the private sector, and other development partners;

- **Tighter social and environmental standards;**

- **Improved fiduciary performance,** through country assessments of financial management and through procurement and fiduciary safeguards at the project level.

The Bank is seeking to build on its experience and adapt approaches as necessary.

Development is a risky business. To develop ideas, the Bank has to take some risks, and some failures are inevitable. What is essential is to learn from those failures. The Bank has done so: for example, by launching a successful Higher Impact Adjustment Lending (HIAL) initiative in Africa in 1995 to improve design and country selection in line with lessons from evaluation; and by changing its approach to the power sector in Africa.

The Bank builds on success by scaling up initiatives that work, such as the high-return dairy cooperative program (Operation Flood) in India. This vast organization grew out of a single, small cooperative society. By 1996, 10 million farmer-members were supplying an average of 11,000 metric tons of milk per day through 55,000 village cooperative societies, and this program and associated policy changes increased the annual growth rate of Indian dairy production from 0.7 to 4.2 percent. In this case, external support from the Bank and others helped to encourage government policy changes that grew out of a homegrown initiative.

The Bank in the late 1990s strengthened its approach to managing by results, and also moved strongly to increase the sharing of knowledge.

In both areas, there has been progress, but there remains considerable room for further improvement.

Effectiveness of global programs

Global interventions are an important complement to country assistance.

Global development challenges—such as the spread of infectious diseases, the challenge of building an international trade and financial architecture, loss of biodiversity, deforestation, and climate change—cannot be handled solely by individual countries and therefore require multilateral action. Such action is typically most effective when linked to country efforts. The Bank has contributed actively to these global programs, through financing, through advocacy, and through alignment with its country programs. Two examples illustrate the far-reaching potential and very large returns of such global initiatives.

- **The West African Onchocerciasis Control Program,** a collaborative effort of multilateral agencies, governments, NGOs, and the private sector. Since it was launched in 1974, the program has eliminated the scourge of riverblindness from 11 countries in West Africa. As a result, it has prevented an estimated 600,000 cases of blindness and added 5 million years of productive labor to the 11 countries' economies.

- **The Consultative Group for International Agricultural Research (CGIAR),** a network of research centers that has created and promoted crop improvements in developing countries over the last 30 years, improving productivity and nutrition, and reducing rural poverty. These centers have produced more than 500 varieties of grain now planted in poor countries and have helped to increase average yields in target grains by 75 percent over three decades.

In recent years, the obvious need for such programs and their strong potential led the Bank to become involved in a growing number of global actions. This in turn led to a greater awareness of the need to maintain focus and tighten priorities. Since 2000, the Bank has moved to make its global programs more strategic by establishing a small number of priority areas for action. This focus has helped increase the resources available for high-priority programs, such as combating AIDS and preventing conflict.

Executive Summary conclusion

Well-allocated foreign aid has been an effective means of supporting poor countries and poor people in their efforts to improve their lives; and with improved allocation and better design and delivery of assistance, aid is more effective today than ever before.

The international development community has recognized that assistance is most effective when recipient countries are the primary drivers of their own reforms and institutional development. Financial aid benefits most the countries that have shown they can use it well. Advice and capacity-building comprise an important complement, especially in the poorest countries and in those that do not have the capacity to absorb significant financial transfers. Advice is often more acceptable and credible when linked to resource transfer.

Since the end of the Cold War, there has been a strong shift in the direction of better allocation of aid, and better tailoring of assistance to country needs and circumstances. Improvement in allocation and the increase in the number of poor countries that are putting in place the governance, institutions, and policies to promote rapid, market-driven, pro-poor growth mean that aid is more effective today than ever before. Yet in the past 10 years, a period when many rich countries experienced remarkable growth, aid allocations have fallen. In inflation-adjusted terms, aid to poor countries was some 7 percent less in 2001 than in 1990. The past record of development progress, and the great efforts the developing countries are now making to develop themselves, provide the evidence that additional aid resources could be used effectively to reduce global poverty.

Introduction

Research staff in the Development Economics Vice Presidency of the World Bank prepared this paper for the United Nations International Conference on Financing for Development held in Monterrey, Mexico, on March 18–22, 2002.[1] It has an ambitious purpose: to analyze in reasonably concise form the changing roles and effectiveness of development assistance during the past 50 years, with particular attention to the past two decades and to the experience of the World Bank. Such a paper cannot possibly be comprehensive. Rather, the authors attempt to describe broadly how the goals and forms of development assistance have changed over time. They conclude that as a result of these changes and, perhaps more important, of improvements in the policies, institutions, and governance of developing countries, aid is more effective at reducing poverty today than ever before.

The past 50 years have taught the international development community—developing countries, donors, and the international financial institutions—a great deal about development and poverty reduction. We now understand better what the goals of development should be and how to attain them. We have learned from both successes and mistakes, in particular about markets, governments, and institutions, and how they interact. This learning—a common and ongoing effort of the entire development community—has led to improved development performance overall and at the World Bank in particular.

At the same time, there is much that we still do not know. Perhaps most important, we do not understand fully how to help improve institutions and governance, especially in the poorest countries where the needs are greatest. And we are still learning how best to deal with pressing cross-border issues that threaten development, such as disease, environmental problems, and political instability.

In recent decades, development has progressed at historically unprecedented rates.[2]

For all the political, economic, and social disruptions of the second half of the 20th century, it was also a period of unprecedented progress in living standards worldwide. Better technology, policies, and institutions not only spurred rapid growth in the advanced economies, they also made possible substantial improvements in the lives of poor people throughout much of the developing world. Progress has been uneven, to be sure. Yet key indicators of well-being testify to striking progress overall.

- **Health.** Over the past 40 years, life expectancy at birth in developing countries has increased by a remarkable 20 years—or about as much as had been achieved in all of human history before the 1960s. The improvement resulted partly from higher incomes and better education, particularly of women and girls, but also in large measure from improved knowledge and understanding about the prevention and treatment of disease, and new programs to share this knowledge and put it into practice.

- **Education.** Over the past 30 years, illiteracy in the developing world has been cut nearly in half, from 47 percent to 25 percent of all adults. Steady expansion of school enrollments worldwide and increases in education quality made key contributions to this improvement, as did improvements in infrastructure and nutrition.

- **Income poverty.** Absolute income poverty—defined as people subsisting on less than $1 per day—rose for much of the past two centuries, but over the past 20 years it has begun to fall. Thanks to better economic policies through much of the developing world—but most importantly in China and India—the number of poor people worldwide appears to have fallen (perhaps by up to 200 million), even as the world's population rose by 1.6 billion.[3] Similarly, a two-century decline in the estimated share of poor people in the global population has accelerated since 1950. In the 1990s alone, the share fell from an estimated 29 percent to 23 percent.[4]

It is impossible to identify with precision the contributions of development assistance to this progress. There is no single agreed approach to doing so, and such assessments face difficulties inherent to the process of assisting a country to develop.

There are various reasons why assessing the contributions of development assistance is inherently difficult. First, responsibility for development progress will always lie primarily with the developing country itself. No outside donor is able, or indeed has the right, to compel a country to follow policies likely to promote development. Nor would it have the local knowledge necessary to do so even if it had the influence. Country ownership of the reform program and development strategy is essential. That is, as the evidence in following sections will show, the country must be committed to and involved in shaping development strategies and projects.

This country ownership is one of several factors making it impossible to assess with any precision the effects of development assistance. If the country takes the lead in reform and institution-building, then by definition the external actor—whether a bilateral donor or a multilateral like the World Bank—plays only a supporting role and should not claim too much of the credit. As discussed in Section 3, other factors also make attribution difficult: the need for partnership across donors, as well as the tendency for the most effective projects to have benefits that extend far beyond the narrow confines of the project itself.

Moreover, levels of development assistance are small relative to other financial flows and to the scale of the challenge at hand. Development aid totaled about $54 billion in 2000; this was only one-third as much as foreign direct investment in developing countries ($167 billion), which itself was only a small fraction of total investment (nearly $1.5 trillion). Similarly, although the World Bank is the world's largest external provider of assistance in the education sector, it typically provides less than $2 billion in direct assistance for education each year.[5] By comparison, annual public spending on education in the developing world totals more than $250 billion. Given this discrepancy in scale, even if the World Bank were to greatly increase its lending in the sector, its effectiveness would have to come primarily through catalyzing institutional development and policy change in education, rather than through resource transfer alone.

This means that the *direct* effects of assistance (for example, in terms of income increases or reductions in mortality) will often be swamped by other factors. Successful development assistance necessarily will have effects that reverberate far beyond the confines of the project itself—either because the ideas are replicated elsewhere, or because the intervention helped to institutionalize new approaches. Yet when the positive effects of aid *do* spill beyond the bounds of the specific project or policy intervention, the effects become much harder to measure.

But while no single type of evidence is definitive, and while there have been problems and disappointments, the evidence suggests that on balance development assistance has contributed strongly to development progress.

Despite these analytic limitations, there is strong evidence that outside assistance is often a powerful force for growth and poverty reduction, provided that the recipient country is committed to using outside resources well. This paper assembles several types of evidence supporting this conclusion. Each of these approaches has methodological problems, and none of them is above challenge. Nevertheless, all four provide evidence that assistance has made a difference, and together they provide a basis for optimism:

- *Cross-country statistical analysis* of the effects of aid, which shows that aid has accelerated growth when allocated correctly, and furthermore, that the allocation of aid by the World Bank and other donors is improving (chapter 3).

- *Project- and sector-level analysis* of specific interventions, drawing primarily on World Bank experience, which shows high returns to development assistance—both in terms of income-focused cost-benefit analysis and in terms of other indicators of human development (chapter 4).

- *Country case studies,* which show that external assistance has played an important role in supporting, cementing, and often helping to shape reform efforts that have delivered massive poverty reduction in recent years, in countries as diverse as Vietnam, Uganda, China, India, Poland, Mozambique, and Bangladesh (boxes in various sections).

- *Evidence on global programs,* which shows that global efforts—such as investment in agricultural research and programs to halt communicable diseases—often have been an important complement to country-specific efforts (chapter 5).

These positive results have depended heavily on learning. The World Bank and other development agencies have adapted their approaches over time, in response not only to changed circumstances but also to lessons learned through experience, research, and evaluation. Some of these are *lessons from successes,* such as those listed above. But the

Bank has also *learned from failures*. For example, it has learned that project lending in poor policy environments typically has much lower returns than in countries with good policies, and that loan conditionality does not alter the policies of recipient countries that are not already committed to change for their own reasons.

This paper focuses on lessons learned and the results that development assistance has already achieved. This is not to suggest there is nothing left to learn. To the contrary, there is much that the global development community and the Bank still do not know. For example, we know too little about how to help countries improve governance and how to support the creation of effective institutions. We also know too little about how to spark reform and growth in the poorest-performing, low-income countries—those that have been mired in a cycle of poor institutions and policies, economic stagnation, and often conflict. The development community recognizes that existing modes of aid and development cooperation have not worked well in these environments. The World Bank, like other development organizations, is now investigating fresh approaches to helping the desperately poor people in these countries.[6]

Continued learning and knowledge are essential to scaling up the fight against poverty.

Despite the progress made in the past 50 years, an immense poverty challenge remains. Some 1.2 billion people still live on less than $1 per day, and the challenge will grow as the population of the developing world increases by another 2 billion in the next 30 years. To address a challenge of these dimensions, aid will need to have effects far beyond the value of the money alone. This means that aid must build the frameworks for private economic activity and social improvements—ensuring that its effects go far beyond any individual project—and it must contribute to greater capacity and greater knowledge. Continued learning is essential to these aims.

1. The Meaning of Development and the Role of Policy, Institutions, and Markets

This chapter provides a brief overview of changes in the way we think about development—what development means, and what approaches will best achieve it.

Ideas about policies and institutions, as well as the policies and institutions themselves, drive development. So understanding how those ideas have evolved, and how they can be changed, is crucial to understanding how we can contribute more effectively to development.

Development thinking has evolved continually over the past 50 years. In response to the lessons of experience and analysis, development practitioners have adapted their approaches to promoting development, and even the goals of development work. We have learned that strategies that seemed obvious to many at some point—for example, both the heavily statist and minimal-government free-market approaches—have had to be reconsidered and changed as part of a continuous learning process. This is one reason why a careful and measured look at experience is so important.

1.1 Objectives for development and development assistance

Early postwar aid was focused on reconstruction of the war-torn economies of Europe and Japan—a task that it contributed to with considerable success.[7] For example, five of the World Bank's first six loans went to countries of Western Europe, and the first four were explicitly for reconstruction. The poor countries of the world were not the first priority, and the focus was on raising production and income, rather than on broader notions of development.

With rapid progress in post-war reconstruction, development assistance began to focus instead on raising incomes in what came to be called the developing world. At first, the goal was largely confined to raising aggregate national incomes. With the recognition that population growth rates vary sharply, so that aggregate income did not necessarily give a clear picture of changes in living standards, attention turned to *per capita* incomes. Soon, however, with increased understanding of issues related to income distribution, simply raising average per capita incomes also was recognized as too limited a goal. By the 1960s and 1970s, attention focused on the twin problems of growth and income distribution and increasingly, on the basic needs of poor people. Reduction of income poverty became a greater priority within the international financial institutions, as well as for governments.

In recent years, the goals of development have come to embrace the elimination of poverty in all its dimensions—income poverty, illiteracy, poor health, insecurity of income, and powerlessness. A consensus is emerging around the view that development means increasing the control that poor people have over their lives, through education, health, and greater participation, as well as income gains. This view comes not only from the testimony of poor people themselves, but also from advances in conceptual thinking about development.[8] It is clear that the various dimensions of poverty are related, and income growth generally leads to strong progress against the nonincome dimensions of poverty as well. It is also clear that direct action to improve these other dimensions can accelerate the reduction of both income and nonincome poverty.

In summary, the objectives of development have evolved in response to changing circumstances and a deeper understanding of poverty. This evolution has made development assistance more complex and challenging. At the same time, it has focused the development community's attention on our essential mission: making it possible for poor people to improve their lives.

1.2 Approaches to development: The roles of states, markets, and institutions[9]

The development community's understanding of the most effective way to achieve development objectives has also evolved over time with the accumulation of evidence and experience. Approaches that appeared at the time to be both correct and obvious have been undermined by experience and closer analysis; in the same way, our current ideas will no doubt give way to others as experience accumulates and thinking evolves. This surely reminds us to beware of simplistic solutions or "silver bullets." Perhaps the most important question on which our understanding has deepened over the past decades is this: what are the respective roles of governments and markets in spurring development, and how do institutions fit into the picture? At the risk of oversimplification, we can identify at least three major phases in the evolution of our answers to these questions.

In practice, we recognize that there is a continuum of approaches, both in developed and developing countries, and that the phases described here do not match precisely the evolution of thinking in any particular region. Instead, they are intended to capture the broad shifts in the thinking of the development community and development practitioners. It is also the case that successful countries throughout this period have seen both state and market play positive roles. With those caveats, this broad-brush portrait can nevertheless provide a useful context for a discussion of development assistance by suggesting where that assistance is most likely to be effective.

Statist and import-substitution period

The 1950s and 1960s were a period of great confidence in government. Development practitioners and thinkers trusted government both for its intentions and for its ability to make economic progress happen, whether in the richer or poorer countries. Development thinking focused on market failures, which were especially prevalent in developing countries and seemed to provide a strong rationale for state intervention. The private sector was thought to be too uncoordinated, too poorly developed, and too focused on private interests to allow it to serve as the locomotive for growth. And in Africa, newly independent countries searched for a post-colonial model of development and a strengthened leadership role for the national state. In many countries around the world, the confidence in government was reflected in the heavy role of central planning and in the relatively closed (import substitution) trade policy.

This state-led approach had some initial development successes. Leading economies of Latin America, where state economic management did not completely crowd out the private sector, grew rapidly for decades under the import-substitution model. And even in some "tiger economies" of East Asia, industry managed to grow and become more productive behind high trade barriers, thanks to otherwise good economic management. Nevertheless, the costs of state economic control became clearer over time. State planners were not omniscient: they could not possibly acquire all the information needed to make decisions that reflected both efficiency considerations and people's differing preferences.

Worse, governments revealed themselves to be collections of interests rather than disinterested and benevolent "social planners." Even had they been effective in their role as social planners, government officials would not have been able to create the entrepreneurial dynamism essential for sustained development and change. Behind protective barriers, firms in many countries (India and Mexico, to name just two) became less efficient as they focused on obtaining government favors rather than improving productivity. Finally, fiscal and macro instability rose with the oil price shocks of the 1970s and early 1980s, contributing to the debt crisis and revealing the weaknesses in the statist model.

Free-market reaction

As a result of the disappointment with the state-led approach, the 1980s and early 1990s saw a strong reaction that stressed the primacy of markets in development. This reaction was a necessary corrective in many ways: it refocused attention on production efficiency and market signals, and it inspired the move to lower trade barriers as a means of spurring productivity. Macro stability and balanced fiscal accounts were seen as fundamental building blocks for development and became early priorities for reform. This period saw substantial improvements in both macro stability and openness through much of the developing world.

At the same time, this school of development thinking also failed to address key points. Once countries began to achieve macro stability and greater openness, it became clear that these were necessary but not sufficient for growth. In particular, the free-market view tended to neglect the institutional foundations of effective private markets. The importance of institutions was underscored by major shifts: the economic decline in the countries of the former Soviet Union; the continued growth in China, a country that moved forward with market-oriented reforms without excessive disruption of institutional foundations; and, later in the 1990s, the financial crisis in East Asia, to which institutional weaknesses contributed heavily. Furthermore, even as it performed a useful service by spotlighting government failure, the free-market reaction had minimized very real problems of market failure that are prevalent in the developing world. As a result, growth performance fell short of expectations in many parts of the developing world.

Deeper understanding of complementarities and role of institutions

Recent years have seen a greater recognition in the policy debate of the complementarities between markets and governments. Clearly, experience shows that the private market economy must be the engine of growth; but it shows also that a vibrant private sector depends on well-functioning state institutions to build a good investment climate and deliver basic services competently.

This view of complementarities draws heavily on what we have learned in the past two to three decades in the more successful cases of income growth, such as East Asia and Chile. It also draws on learning from the transition process in the former Soviet Union, where a lack of institutional development combined with excessively optimistic expectations led to extremely disappointing development outcomes and demonstrated clearly the importance of a sound state in providing the environment for growth. The role of institutions has come through more strongly than it did in earlier views of development, and particularly than it did in the policy debate in the 1980s and early 1990s. As Section 2.3 shows, countries that have combined institutional improvements with market-oriented policy reforms and greater engagement with the world economy saw their per capita incomes grow in the 1990s at the very rapid pace of 5 percent per year.

Continued learning

This understanding of states, markets, and institutions has strong conceptual foundations, and it is based also in experience with what works in development. There is a strong and growing consensus about the value of such an approach. Nevertheless, there is much that the development community has yet to learn. The World Bank is committed to continued learning and to constant improvements in our overall approach to development. For example, while institutions have now taken a central role in the World Bank's strategic approach to development, we are keenly aware that we know far too little about just how to build them.[10]

1.3 Summary

We have learned a great deal about what development means and how, broadly, to achieve it.

Our understanding of what development means has evolved. Poverty reduction efforts should **address poverty in all its dimensions**—lack of income, but also the lack of health and education, the vulnerability to shocks, and the lack of control over their lives that poor people suffer. This multidimensionality of poverty reduction is embodied in the Millennium Development Goals.

We have also learned more about the most effective broad model for development:

- Evidence from past successes and failures suggests strongly that neither the more statist approach of the 1950s and 1960s nor the more minimal-government free-market approach that dominated policy debate in the 1980s and early 1990s will achieve these goals.

- Effective approaches will be led by the private sector, but with effective government to provide the governance framework and to ensure the provision of physical infrastructure and human capital investments necessary for growth and poverty reduction. In fact, to set state and market against each other is to miss the central question: how can they best complement each other to promote growth and reduce poverty?

- A public-private development partnership is essential, especially in the area of health and education. Institutional development has too often been neglected in the development policy debate, but is now recognized to be essential to sustained poverty reduction.

2. Sources of Growth and Poverty Reduction

The development community has learned much about the sources of growth and poverty reduction.

Development depends on two pillars, which together support sustained growth and poverty reduction:

- Countries must *build a good investment climate*—an environment in which the private sector will invest and produce efficiently, in a way that generates jobs and productivity growth. The investment climate consists of all the factors that most influence private-sector decisions: macroeconomic stability and openness, governance and institutions, and infrastructure. The "private sector" should be understood not only (or even primarily) to include large firms and multinationals, but also farmers and small and medium enterprises (SMEs).

- Countries must *empower and invest in poor people,* so that they can participate in growth. We know that sustained growth is essential for poverty reduction, so the investment climate focus is itself a tool for poverty reduction. At the same time, governments need to target poverty more directly, notably by equipping poor people with the tools necessary to contribute to growth, such as education and health, and by giving them access to infrastructure and financial services. People are empowered when they are given the ability to shape their own lives, whether through greater capabilities or through participation in decisionmaking. Direct actions by government, international organizations, and NGOs are necessary to help this happen.

Many countries have built up these two pillars in recent decades and have seen the rewards: rapid growth and poverty reduction. Although too many other countries continue to fall behind economically, a majority of the developing world's population lives in countries that have grown rapidly and are closing the gap with the rich countries. Even the countries that have stagnated economically have, for the most part, seen material improvements in social indicators, such as health and education measures.

Development assistance has helped accelerate this progress. It aims at helping countries build both pillars: improving the investment climate (through building the factors that contribute to investment and growth), and empowering people (through education, health, and social protection). Chapter 2 explicates the context for development assistance, by laying out in greater detail the channels through which assistance can affect growth—that is, the factors that give rise to growth and poverty reduction. It also summarizes the success and failure of countries at generating growth. Chapters 3 through 5 below show that these efforts have had large rewards.

2.1 What drives the growth of GDP and productivity?

Approaches: Understanding sources of growth[11]

To increase incomes, countries need to improve one or both of two fronts:

- They can rely on **factor accumulation:** that is, they can accumulate more of the factors of production, such as physical capital (through investment) and human capital (through higher levels of education and health among the population).

- They can increase what economists call **total factor productivity (TFP)**—the efficiency with which these factors produce output. TFP represents both the quality of the policy and institutional environment, on the one hand, and knowledge and technology on the other.

In practice, virtually all sustained growth processes involve some combination of factor accumulation and increased productivity, with the respective shares of the two varying across countries and time periods. In any event, the real world usually defies a clean breakdown into these two factors; the question of how effectively inputs are used enters not just into productivity, but also into the accumulation of capital. Many development interventions are aimed at accelerating both factor accumulation and productivity growth.

Our understanding of the sources of growth of GDP and productivity is based on several types of research: cross-country regressions, growth decompositions, case studies, and microeconomic studies of the sources of productivity growth. All these approaches have their shortcomings. For example, regressions and growth decompositions are ways of assembling statistically aggregate indicators and trying to identify the most important explanatory factors. Yet while these methods reveal associations between statistical variables, they cannot prove that one factor causes another. Moreover, they place excessive emphasis on a simplistic aggregate production function model of accumulation and production. Much of the growth comes from reallocation of resources to more dynamic sectors; from different ways of organizing productive activity; and from intensification of entrepreneurship. None of these are illuminated by the aggregate production function approach.

The results from country case studies do not suffer from these weaknesses, but they may be too country specific to provide lessons by themselves for other countries. Nevertheless, together these methods sketch out a good picture of what matters in spurring overall income growth. While no single variable stands up as a determinant of growth in all analyses of growth processes, certain factors appear to be particularly important; these are discussed below.

Broadly, it is clear that private-sector growth is essential to long-term development. While the state can have some success in financing or inducing factor accumulation over the medium term, it is far less successful at inducing productivity growth when it takes a lead role in the economy. Even when a state-dominated economy manages large quantities of investment, the quality of that investment is often low. Moreover, employment provides the main long-term route out of poverty, but the vast majority of the world's poor workers are employed in the private sector, not the public sector. Moreover, few of these private-sector jobs are in large firms; most of the world's poorest people work in small firms, most notably small farms. For these reasons, any development strategy must have at its core a focus on building a good climate for private-sector investment, productivity, and employment creation by all firms, small and large.

Given this background, which factors most affect long-term economic growth and poverty reduction? Although different analysts will have somewhat different lists, most would agree on many of the factors listed below. One way to organize these factors is to group them in terms of the major elements of the investment climate that are amenable to direct action by governments: macro factors such as macroeconomic stability and trade openness; governance and institutions, including basic service delivery in education; and infrastructure. Geography is an additional factor that cannot be directly influenced by policy but can have important effects on growth and development.

Macro factors—macroeconomic stability and openness—are important drivers of growth.

Macroeconomic stability. Unstable fiscal accounts and high inflation undermine the private sector by reducing predictability and discouraging investment.[12] The slowing of growth rates in much of the developing world after the 1960s and early 1970s stemmed in part from macroeconomic instability, which reduced confidence in government and in its ability to maintain a stable climate for productivity, jobs, and growth. While macro stability on its own is not enough to jump start growth and development, it is generally a prerequisite for sustained progress.

International trade and investment.[13] There remains some debate about the degree of trade liberalization that is advisable for poorer developing countries—debate fueled by the observation that open domestic markets were not a precondition for rapid growth in the East Asian tigers, nor indeed historically in much of Europe and North America. Yet it is also clear that most recent periods of rapid growth have also been periods of increased engagement with the international economy. In the 1990s, for example, developing countries that had fast export growth also had, on average, 1 percent higher annual growth in GDP than those with slow export growth; in the 1980s, the difference was even greater.[14] The domestic investment climate and the actions of the domestic private sector are the key drivers of development, but international engagement can play an important complementary role. Even in historically closed economies such as China, which was far from completely open during the early reform period, high growth was fueled in part by increased access to international capital and markets. Where local conditions for entrepreneurship and growth are good, exposure to international competition increases the productivity of domestic firms and lowers input costs for downstream users, while foreign direct investment brings with it new production and process technologies, organizational capacity-building, and marketing networks.

Micro and structural factors—governance, education, and other elements of the investment climate—also play a big role in generating growth.

Physical capital investment. Many of the early analyses in the empirical growth literature found that the level of investment in physical capital plays a role in determining growth rates.[15] But subsequent empirical research, together with the anecdotal experience of countries that achieved high investment rates but slow productivity growth (such as the Soviet Union), has shifted attention from quantity to quality and productivity of investment. Factor accumulation by itself leaves much to be explained in growth regressions, and the evidence is that total factor productivity growth—which captures quality improvement—explains a major share of most episodes of long-term economic growth.[16] The lesson is that we need to focus on the investment climate: the constellation of underlying factors causing growth of productive investment.[17]

Human capital investment through education and health. It is widely thought that an educated and healthy workforce also contributes to growth, with widespread basic education (primary and secondary) being especially important.[18] Not all empirical analyses find such an effect. One reason that the effects of education have been hard to pin down empirically is that the quality of education matters as much as the quantity, and yet we are much better at measuring quantity than quality. Another reason is that, like physical capital, human capital may be relatively unproductive from a societal standpoint if a weak investment climate inhibits development.[19] But while the case is not fully established empirically, strong basic education and reasonable levels of health have been a precursor to many development successes, and recent analyses suggest strongly that additional education does indeed spur development in the typical country. Finally, as discussed below, the evidence on the substantial returns to education at the microeconomic level is unambiguous: education lifts people out of poverty, raising their earnings by some 5 to 10 percent per year of schooling.

Sound institutions, governance, and rule of law. Stable and effective government institutions, respect for property rights, equal treatment under the law, the absence of bureaucratic harassment, a lack of corruption, and protection from organized crime all matter for growth. Investment and productivity depend on predictability, which in turn hinges on confidence that government will not act opportunistically or capriciously. The "soft infrastructure" of an effective legal and judicial system is critical, whether for achieving economic growth, empowerment of poor people, or security. Good governance also reduces the costs faced by producers. Sound supervision and regulation of financial institutions decreases the costs of capital to businesses and contributes greatly to macroeconomic stability.[20] Indeed, it has been argued that institutional quality and governance are the underlying variables that drive all of the other growth-enhancing factors.[21]

Gender equality and social inclusion. Recent research provides evidence that gender equality—not only in health and education, but also in voice and rights—is an important element in development.[22] Aside from the obvious direct benefits for women, equality in these dimensions also has instrumental benefits in terms of growth and poverty reduction. Cross-country research suggests that low investment in female education has been a barrier to growth in South Asia, Sub-Saharan Africa, and the Middle East and North Africa, compared with East Asia, which closed the gender gap more rapidly. And even after controlling for income and other factors, more equal rights and greater participation by women in public life is associated with cleaner business and government and better governance, which in turn promotes growth. Inequalities along other dimensions—such as race, ethnicity, or religion—can also retard development.

Competition. Vibrant competition is important in spurring productivity growth. Interventions that increase the extent of the market, including good domestic infrastructure, reduce costs and improve the selection of goods and services by widening the number of competitors. The dynamic effects of such changes, which work through the increased productivity growth they spur, may greatly exceed the one-time benefits to consumers of accessing goods from new suppliers at lower prices.[23] Competitive pressures can come through various means. Openness to imports is often the most effective source of competition—and the one that requires least administrative capacity on the part of government—but other important sources have included well-functioning competition authorities and government-mandated "export tournaments."[24] Ensuring that firms can both enter and exit markets is also an important element of competition.

Infrastructure. Physical infrastructure also matters a great deal in terms of both investment climate and empowerment. Transportation and communications infrastructure connect markets and people, both domestically and internationally.[25] Better infrastructure thus diminishes the effects of geography, reducing costs to producers and improving the reach of government and private services for consumers. In Sri Lanka, for example, the arrival of telephone service in rural areas increased farmers' share of the price crops sold in the capital city from 50 to 60 percent to 80 to 90 percent.[26] In Peru, households with access to modern infrastructure (water, sanitation, electricity, and telecommunications) had income growth about 45 percent higher than households without these services.[27] Availability of affordable and reliable energy supplies is another important spur to production, while good water and sewage infrastructure improves health and environmental outcomes. How government can best provide infrastructure, or facilitate its provision by the private sector, is a key question for development assistance, as are the questions of the prioritization and sequencing of infrastructure investment.

Geography. Geography seriously impedes growth for some countries, making development much more difficult.[28] If a country is landlocked, mountainous, and surrounded by poor neighbors, or if its population centers are in remote areas, it may encounter additional difficulties in developing domestic markets of efficient size, engaging in international trade, or acquiring technology from abroad. In such cases, it will be especially important to build effective infrastructure links, to improve transportation and communications both domestically and internationally. Regional integration and trade-creating customs unions may also be important in overcoming geographic barriers. Ecological fragility is another geography-linked barrier to development: ecological stresses may most directly affect poor people, and these stresses too require specific policy and institutional responses.

Putting these factors together to spur sustained growth is a challenge: it requires proper sequencing and selection of reforms, as well as consistency over time, neither of which is easy to achieve.

Although our understanding of the importance of these factors has grown over time, to put them together in a way that yields sustained growth remains a daunting challenge. One major challenge for governments is to decide where to focus their efforts as they strive to make the conditions for growth as favorable as possible. Strategies have to be determined in each country context, but it is clear that administrative capacities of low-income governments are typically so limited that an assessment of where they should be focused is essential: the government simply cannot push ahead effectively on all fronts at once. At the same time, sequencing is necessary. It is by now widely recognized that the East Asian financial crisis of 1997–98, which exacted a substantial cost in poverty and lost output, stemmed in no small measure from financial and capital-market liberalization that proceeded before the appropriate regulatory safeguards were in place. But while some sequencing problems are easier to identify, finding the best sequencing of steps in a particular country context is a great challenge, and it remains an area where our knowledge needs to expand further.

Another major challenge is sustaining growth. Rapid growth episodes of a few years or a decade are not uncommon. For example, countries that successfully emerge from civil war often experience relatively rapid economic rebounds for several years.[29] What has been much less common is sustained rapid growth over a period of decades, which is what is necessary to eliminate absolute poverty.[30]

The need for consistency underlines the importance of attaining sustained productivity growth. Only a portion of growth is driven by increases in physical and human-capital intensity of production, which can be difficult to sustain over long periods. Countries also need rapid growth in productivity.

2.2 What factors drive poverty reduction?

The World Bank and its partners—United Nations agencies, bilateral donors, and governments—have committed to a common set of poverty-reduction results, including the Millennium Development Goals agreed to by governments at major conferences in the 1990s. The goals are accompanied by numerical targets expressed in terms of changes between 1990 and 2015: reducing the share of people living in poverty worldwide by half; reducing infant and child mortality by two-thirds; reducing maternal mortality by three-quarters and improving access to reproductive health services; and halting the increase in incidence of communicable diseases (AIDS, malaria, TB) and reducing malnutrition. What do we know about the factors underlying the reduction of poverty, in both its income and social dimensions? [31]

Growth and poverty reduction

Economic growth is essential for sustained progress on poverty reduction. Countries that have reduced income poverty the most are those that have grown the fastest, and poverty has grown fastest in countries that have stagnated economically. Between 1992 and 1998, for example, the share of the population in poverty fell an average of 5 to 8 percent annually in fast-growing Uganda, India, Vietnam, and China.[32] In Nigeria, by contrast, per capita consumption fell 16 percent between 1992 and 1996, and the poverty share increased by half, from 43 percent to 66 percent of the population.[33]

Income distribution and poverty reduction

Some have expressed fear that growth alone cannot be relied upon to result in significant poverty reduction in developing countries. Evidence shows that income distribution has not changed on average in periods of growth in the typical country, and that therefore overall growth has meant that the incomes of the poor have increased (again, on average) proportionately. In China, inequality did increase with reform; but the increase in inequality was an inevitable feature of the improvement in the incentive structure, which led to growth and poverty reduction. Indeed, growth was so strong that poverty fell sharply despite worsening income distribution. In other cases—Uganda, for example—income distribution improved at least modestly with reforms and growth.[34]

Nevertheless, it is the case that countries with better income distribution see growth translate into faster poverty reduction. At the same rate of GDP growth, a country with highly equal distribution (that is, one with a Gini coefficient of 0.30) will see poverty fall twice as fast as a highly unequal country (Gini of 0.60).[35] In addition, the evidence suggests that greater inequality of important assets, such as land and education, may retard societywide growth.

It is also the case that groups of poor people will experience reform and growth differently. A large increase in the income of one group may be offset by a smaller increase or even decline in the income of another group.[36] This underlines the importance of ensuring that there is adequate social protection in place as a complement to structural adjustment measures. Social protection helps build broader support for action, and it enables individuals to take risks involved in entrepreneurship. And social protection is not just an instrument for achieving growth: it also targets poverty directly, by reducing the income vulnerability that poor people identify as one of the defining elements of a life in poverty.[37]

Determinants of improved social indicators

Once we recognize that poverty is about more than income, we see that there are other determinants of poverty reduction beyond growth. Social indicators—health and education—improved far faster in the 20th century than we would have expected, given the rate of income growth. Most countries have made major progress in increasing educational attainment and health outcomes by targeting these goals directly, and by applying new knowledge and technologies, rather than just waiting for the effects of income growth to improve these indicators. At every level of income, infant mortality fell sharply during the 20th century. For example, a typical country with per-capita income of $8,000 in 1950 (measured in 1995 dollars) would have had, on average, an infant mortality rate of 45 per 1,000 live births. By 1970, a country at the same real income level would typically have had an infant mortality rate of only 30 per 1,000; by 1995, only 15 per 1,000.[38] Similar reductions occurred all along the income spectrum, including in the poorest countries.

The improvements in social indicators are remarkable by historical standards. As noted in the preface, life expectancy in developing countries increased by 20 years over a period of only 40 years, as it shot from the mid-40s to the mid-60s. By comparison, it probably took millennia to improve life expectancy from the mid-20s to the mid-40s. Literacy improvements have also been remarkable: whereas in 1970 nearly two out of every four adults were illiterate, now it is only one out of every four.

These advances in education and health have greatly improved the welfare of individuals and families. Not only are education and health valuable in themselves, but they also increase income-earning capacity. Where macroeconomic analyses of the growth effects of education have been somewhat ambiguous, the microeconomic evidence of the returns to education is overwhelming and robust. Each additional year of education increases the average individual worker's wages by at least 5 to 10 percent.[39] And educating women is a particularly effective way to raise the human development levels of children. Mothers who are more educated have healthier children, even at a given level of income. They are also more productive in the labor force, which raises household incomes and thereby increases child survival rates—in part because, compared with men, women tend to spend additional income in ways that benefit children more.

These trends make it clear that public policy matters. Government has a role not only in ensuring delivery of good basic services in health and education, but also in ensuring that technology and knowledge spread widely through the economy. The dramatic improvement in life expectancy at a given income level is attributable to environmental changes and is the result of public health actions. The control of diarrheal diseases, including the development of oral rehydration therapy to reduce child mortality, is one example; the education of women was an important component of these efforts. Smallpox eradication, made possible through a combination of advances in public health research and effective program management, is another example of a successful 20th century public health effort.

Bangladesh (see box 2.1) provides an excellent example of a country that has expanded educational access and improved neonatal and reproductive health dramatically and unexpectedly in a short time. Growth has not been rapid, although it has increased in each decade since independence, and Bangladesh has suffered from weak governance. However, because Bangladesh has taken targeted steps to achieve health and educational goals and has provided a framework for dynamic NGOs to fight poverty, the country has achieved much in a short time. As the box explains, the World Bank and other donors provided important analytical and financial support.

Box 2.1. Improving Health through Direct Action in Bangladesh

Bangladesh, one of the poorest, most densely populated countries in the world, has made remarkable progress in improving the health and education of its people since its independence in 1971. It has done so thanks to a partnership between the government, donors, and other partners, with local nongovernmental organizations (NGOs) playing a central driving role throughout the period. Since it established its office in Bangladesh in 1972, the World Bank has also contributed strongly to these efforts.

Over the past 30 years, Bangladesh has seen infant mortality drop from about 140 to 71 per 1,000 live births, and is the only one among the world's 20 poorest countries to record a sustained reduction in birth rates over the past 20 years. The country has also achieved outstanding progress in basic education, with most children now attending primary school and nearly a third attending secondary school. Progress in girls' education

continued

Box 2.1. Improving Health through Direct Action in Bangladesh (continued)

stands out: the proportion of primary school students who are girls increased from 37 percent in 1980 to virtual parity with boys in 1995. Girls' enrollment as a percentage of total secondary enrollment has increased dramatically from 34 percent in 1990 to 48 percent in 1997.

The World Bank's dialogue with Bangladesh on health and population issues began in 1973, when the Bank helped mobilize support from six cofinanciers for a project. Since then, additional donors have been engaged in follow-up projects, each of which has almost doubled the amount of money invested. A series of World Bank Population and Health projects over the years has led to a marked increase in the use of contraceptives and decreases in infant mortality in Bangladesh. At the close of the Population and Health IV project (a $180 million implemented between 1991 and 1998), Bangladesh was nearing complete national coverage of family planning and limited primary health care services by community health workers.

In education, the World Bank has funded 14 projects in Bangladesh worth $691 million, covering technical, vocational, primary, and female education. Projects have supported low-cost school construction, strengthening teacher training, improving the design of textbooks, and revamping the curriculum. They have emphasized a role for communities to support schools in their villages. With the large increases in the number of children in school, recent projects have focused on enhancing the quality of learning.

In 1993, the World Bank financed a groundbreaking Female Secondary School Assistance Project, which was aimed at increasing female enrollment and completion. The project supported a government program to provide stipends and cover all school-related costs for girls. The program the project supported resulted in large increases in female enrollments, delays in the age of marriage, a higher number of single-child families, improved birth spacing, and more females employed with higher incomes.

The World Bank is continuing its work in health and education. Current education projects are helping to improve quality of primary education and provide opportunities to newly literate adults, and a second Female Secondary School Assistance project is in the pipeline. In health, the Bank is playing a lead role in helping to coordinate donors in the government's sectorwide approach to health and population development.

Similarly, Mexico has achieved substantial improvements in the educational attainment and health of its poor citizens through its Progresa program, which it launched on its own, without donor support (see box 2.2). The program has been so successful that it is being emulated in a number of other countries, with Bank advisory and financial support. A third major example, discussed in chapter 5, is the Onchocerciasis Control Program, which has virtually eliminated riverblindness in 11 countries of West Africa.

Box 2.2. Mexico's Homegrown Program Helps Poor People Invest in Schooling and Health

Starting in 1996, and working without direct involvement from international agencies, the Mexican government designed and successfully implemented Progresa, a program to provide immediate financial transfers to the rural poor that at the same time promotes investment in children's human capital via increased schooling and improved health and nutrition status. Progresa provides cash transfers (grants) to poor rural families conditional on keeping children in school and providing them with basic preventive health care and nutrition. A key feature of the program is the provision of the transfer to mothers, a mechanism designed to ensure that the money is invested in children and which also serves to empower women in rural communities. In 2001, Progresa accounted for just 2.3 percent of the government's social expenditures, or 0.2 percent of GDP. Impressive results (during 1996–1999) from external evaluation (carried out by IFPRI) make it clear that the program is reaching its intended beneficiaries:

- Progresa provided benefits to 2.6 million poor rural families (or over half of rural families) in 2000. In 2001, the program is expected to cover 3.2 million families in more than 55,000 communities with high poverty rates throughout 2,200 rural municipalities of the country.

- Education grants are supporting schooling for 3.6 million poor children (2.3 million at the primary level and 1.3 million at secondary level). Nutrition and health grants are benefiting 1.6 million children aged 0 to 5 years of age, and 0.8 million pregnant and lactating women, respectively.

continued

Box 2.2. Mexico's Homegrown Program Helps Poor People Invest in Schooling and Health (continued)

And Progresa is achieving results by increasing educational attainment and improving health:

- It raised secondary enrollment rates by 8 percent for girls and 5 percent for boys, and slightly increased the already high primary enrollment rates. It is estimated that children's educational achievement has increased by about 10 percent, which would represent an increase in their future earnings of over 8 percent.

- It increased prenatal care in the first trimester of pregnancy in 8 percent of cases, and decreased the incidence of disease among children under 5 by 12 percent among program participants. Progresa achieved a comparable decline in the probability of malnutrition among children aged 12 to 36 months.

Similar programs for conditional cash transfers to poor families, linked to participation in education (and, in many cases, health) programs are now being implemented widely in Latin America and the Caribbean, including Brazil, Colombia, and Jamaica, as well as in Turkey.

2.3 Within this picture of strong development at the global level, we find divergent country experiences with growth and poverty reduction.

Within the overall picture of global development progress, the experiences of various developing regions and countries have differed sharply. Some countries have grown very rapidly, others hardly at all in recent decades. Figure 2.1 provides an illustration of this, graphing median per-capita incomes from 1970 to 2000 for two groups of developing countries—ten of the fastest-growing and ten of the slowest-growing countries.[40] The divergence over that period has been extraordinary: while the median "high group" country has nearly quadrupled the average income of its people over 30 years, the slow-growing countries now find their people some 40 percent poorer on average than they were at the start of the period. Comparisons of individual countries make the same point: The Republic of Korea had a lower nominal GDP per capita than Ghana in 1960 ($155 versus $180). However, because of Korea's growth, its average nominal income is now 35 times that of

Figure 2.1. Long-Term Effects of Growth and Stagnation in 20 Countries

Index of per capita
GDP (1970=100)

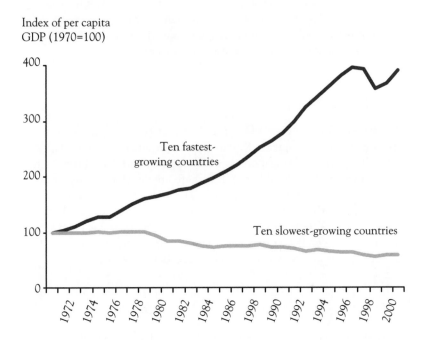

Ghana—even though Ghana is not among the world's slowest-growing economies.

The excellent health achievements also hide regional and country divergences. Like income growth, improvements in health status and life expectancy have not been equally distributed. The health status and life expectancy of the poorest nations lag behind the rest of the world, and within countries, the health of the poor is worse than that of the rest of the population. Poverty is the most important underlying cause of preventable death, disease, and disability; and there is growing recognition that poor health, malnutrition, and large family size are key determinants of poverty.[41]

The overall picture for the developing world of course lies in between these two groups, but in strongly positive territory. Since 1965, the per-capita GDP of the developing world as a whole has increased by an average of 2.2 percent per year, more than doubling the income of the average developing-country resident. Again, this is a huge change by historical standards.[42] And since 1990, developing countries have on average grown faster in per capita terms than the richer countries. Given the good policies that developing countries have been putting in place, we should expect this catch-up to continue.

Successful historical cases

The development success of countries of East Asia, starting with the "tiger economies" of Japan, Korea, Taiwan province of China, Hong Kong (China), and Singapore, is widely known and does not need to be recapitulated in detail here.[43] But there are developing countries outside of East Asia, such as Botswana, that also have a consistent record of growth and poverty reduction over several decades. And other countries that are now high-income, such as Portugal and Ireland, achieved this status by growing more rapidly than other OECD countries over the past several decades.

More recent successes

A substantial number of countries, with a very large share of the developing world's population, have grown very rapidly and reduced poverty in the last two decades. One group of 24 countries that sharply increased the trade intensity of their economies since the 1970s has seen per capita incomes increase by an average of 5 percent per year in the 1990s. These countries are home to 3 billion of the developing world's 5 billion people, and such rapid growth in relatively large countries is responsible for the global progress in reducing absolute poverty. (For comparison, the rich countries grew at just 2 percent per year.) Even with fast-growing China excluded, per capita incomes in the remaining countries—such as Mexico, Thailand, Hungary, and Indonesia—grew an average of 3.5 percent per year. By historical standards, this is a very rapid growth pace, fast enough to double incomes in just two decades.[44]

Policy reforms and institution-building have driven much of this growth. Greater integration with international markets was one factor, but by no means the only one, or even necessarily the most important. In most cases, growth came only with improvements in the broader investment climate: macro stability as well as greater openness, but also better governance, institutions, and infrastructure. (Box 2.3 discusses the World Bank supportive role in reforms that spurred rapid growth in India, and the role of external assistance in that country's growth and development.)

Indeed, the 1980s and 1990s were periods of major policy reforms throughout the developing world. We can see this clearly, for example, in the areas of macro stability and openness. The median inflation rate of developing countries was cut in half between 1982 and 1997, from about 15 to 7 percent. In low-income countries, the improvements were even greater. More important, at the end of the 1990s only 5 percent of developing countries had inflation above 10 percent. Average tariff rates have also declined sharply in all developing regions. In

---

Box 2.3. The World Bank's Role in India: Support for Policy Reforms, Analysis, and Demonstration Projects

India throughout the 1960s and 1970s was weakly integrated into the international economy, and internally it relied heavily on physical planning and licensing. As a result, its rates of economic growth and poverty reduction were unimpressive. Though its growth accelerated in the 1980s, the growth was based largely on unsustainable public spending and foreign borrowing. This led to a fiscal and balance of payments crisis and a new, reformist government in 1991. The IMF and the World Bank helped the government to design and implement fiscal and trade reforms to stabilize and open up the economy. The work of the Bank has been of particular significance in India's decentralization over the last half-decade, which has required the World Bank to work more and more closely with state, local, and municipal governments. The Bank opted to focus its advice and finance on several key reforming states to ensure that fiscal and structural reforms work well, lead to growth, poverty reduction, and improved social indicators, and have powerful demonstration effects for lagging states. Probably the Bank's most influential work in India has been in the social and agricultural sectors, but the Bank has also provided timely advice and financial assistance for power sector reforms in several Indian states. In the early 1990s, the Bank was an early proponent of restructuring and privatization as the solution to the chronic bankruptcy, inefficiency, and shortages that characterize India's power sector. Now the Bank is working with a half-dozen states on power sector restructuring, with the support of the central government and other partners.

continued

79

Box 2.3. The World Bank's Role in India: Support for Policy Reforms, Analysis, and Demonstration Projects (continued)

In addition to its policy-based work, the World Bank supports small-scale projects with high demonstration effects. For example, we launched a land reclamation project in Uttar Pradesh in 1993 that, to date, has involved more than 85,000 families and has reversed the alkaline salts degradation of 47,000 hectares. The benefits go well beyond reclaimed land: previously landless families have received land titles (jointly, in the name of the wife as well as husband), farmers have learned new sustainable techniques, women have been empowered through self-help groups that operate small credit and saving schemes, and family incomes have increased by almost 50 percent. The project model is so successful that the government of Uttar Pradesh plans to follow it in all future sodic land reclamation. Similar stories could be told about innovative work undertaken in close collaboration with the Bank, and subsequently mainstreamed by the Government of India, in sectors as diverse as elementary education and rural water supply. In elementary education, the District Primary Education Program—initiated in 1995 with support from the Bank and a consortium of donors, and covering 15 of the country's 29 states—has now been extended across the country by the government through its new Education for All program. In rural water supply, the Indian government adopted in 1998 a new demand-driven, community-based policy, which was very much influenced by Bank pilot projects. Twenty percent of central government funds are now allocated to states implementing sectoral reforms which are designed in ways which reflect the Bank's direction of supportive efforts.

When the government has been committed to reform, World Bank analytical work, together with that of others, has played an influential supporting role. The Bank's timely analytical work on trade policies helped the government in the late 1980s and early 1990s, as it began to dismantle the highly protectionist regime then in place. More recently, the Bank has been collaborating with the Confederation of Indian Industries on a survey of private firms to assess India's investment climate in terms of bottlenecks, corruption, harassment, and infrastructure weaknesses. The results of this work have already been widely disseminated and quoted in the press, and have added momentum to the government's efforts to dismantle the planning apparatus in India, particularly at the state level. Recent work in health and pensions is having a similar impact on policy debate.

South Asia, for example, the unweighted average fell from about 65 percent in 1980–85 to 30 percent in 1996–98; in Latin American and the Caribbean, from 30 percent to under 15 percent. Tariff averages are an imperfect measure of openness, but there have been even greater declines in the black-market exchange-rate premium, which is an indicator of macroeconomic instability as well as of the restrictiveness of the trade regime.[45]

Aid indicators of success

Another way of gauging development success is to look at the numbers of graduates from the World Bank's soft- and hard-loan windows (IDA lending at concessional terms and IBRD lending at nonconcessional terms, respectively). We are not suggesting here or elsewhere that the Bank alone was responsible for these improvements; on the contrary, the Bank has, at best, supported countries' own efforts and those of others. Twenty-three countries have seen their incomes increase to the point that they could graduate from IDA and remain IDA graduates, borrowing only from IBRD at nonconcessional terms. (A few others graduated from IDA but later had to return, because their economic performance had worsened and their creditworthiness for IBRD lending became limited.) In addition, 26 countries have graduated from IBRD. This includes Korea, which had started as a low-income IDA borrower but graduated from IBRD lending in 1994.[46] About ten IBRD-eligible countries have developed to the extent that they have gained broad, though volatile, access to international capital markets. Most of these countries have stopped borrowing from the Bank for extended periods in which they have had good access to commercial financing, but continue to value Bank support during periods in which they are buffeted by external shocks. They also continue to draw on the Bank for advisory and other nonfinancial services.

Lagging countries

Not all countries have been this successful. Indeed, the number of countries that have grown slowly or stagnated over the past two decades is larger than the group of rapid integrators listed above, although the total population of these poor-performing countries is less than that of the more successful countries.[47] Most notably, Sub-Saharan Africa as a region saw no increase in its per-capita incomes between 1965 and 1999, even with improved performance in the 1990s. And although Africa did make steady progress on health and education indicators over much of that period, despite the lack of income growth, the progress in increasing life expectancy has been reversed by the AIDS epidemic in many countries, as well as by malaria and tuberculosis.[48]

The economic decline in much of Sub-Saharan Africa stems in part from events beyond African countries' control, including large and persistent declines in the prices of their export commodities. For example, non-oil exporters in Africa (other than South Africa) lost a cumulative 120 percent of their GDP between 1970 and 1997 as a result of changes in import and export prices. In addition, Africa has faced geographic challenges and protected export markets, as well as many investors' reluctance to change their risk perceptions of the continent.

However, it is not only external factors that explain Africa's weak performance. Numerous shortcomings in domestic governance, weaknesses in institutions, and misdirected policies and investments have also contributed. Too many African countries have suffered from an investment climate that has not proven conducive to growth and productivity.[49] And mistakes by donors sometimes compounded these problems, as discussed in chapter 3.

In many of the lagging countries, there are now encouraging signs of progress. Over the past decade, and especially in the past five years, Sub-Saharan Africa has achieved very significant improvements in macroeconomic stability and governance, including widespread democratization. For example, the median inflation rate has fallen from 12 percent in 1990 to 4 percent in 2000. In 1990, 15 countries had negative growth rates, and only 17 countries had growth rates greater than 3 percent. By 2000, only 8 countries had negative growth rates, while 22 had growth rates greater than 3 percent. Perhaps most remarkable among these improvements is the peaceful transition from apartheid to democracy in South Africa and that country's transition from hyperinflation to macro stability.

The New Partnership for African Development (NEPAD), proposed by several governments in the region, reflects a welcome recognition of the importance of domestic responsibility. It calls for a partnership in which domestic reforms will be supported by increased external assistance, including debt relief and in reductions in protectionist trade policies in rich countries. The Bank, along with many others, welcomed this partnership and is committed to working with African leaders and other partners in ensuring that the next decade does indeed see a broad-based turnaround in Africa's disappointing development record.

The mixed experience of transition

In Eastern Europe and the former Soviet Union, the experience of transition from a centrally planned to a market economy has varied greatly across countries.[50] Every country went through a "transition recession" before output began to recover, but the depth and length of those recessions differed. Countries in Eastern Europe—helped by prior experience of markets and nationhood, and buoyed by the prospect of accession to the European Union—more quickly followed policies to downsize unprofitable enterprises and encourage rapid entry of new firms. This policy package led to deep recessions, but these economies began to recover after several years of decline, and output exceeded its pretransition levels by 2000. Today, the countries of Central Europe and the Baltics have made considerable progress with market-oriented reforms, to the point where they are poised for early accession to the European Union. (See box 2.4 for a discussion of the transformation in a top-performing transition country, Poland.)

In contrast, the countries of the former Soviet Union experienced a prolonged recession, much deeper than the Great Depression. The severity of the recession stemmed from various factors. The dissolution of the Soviet Union, where industrialization had been based on cheap energy and subsidized transport, disrupted production and trade relationships. CIS countries also lacked any recent memory of market economies, and in a number of cases, they suffered from war and civil strife. With the exception of the Baltics, where output recovered rapidly despite the deep initial recession, vested private interests captured the state in most CIS countries early in the transition. The CIS also failed to stop fiscal and financial leakage to unprofitable enterprises and to discipline managers by developing and strengthening institutions of corporate governance. The result was large-scale corruption that undermined confidence in reforms. These countries also failed to put in place policies that would encourage new firms that can create wealth and contribute to economic growth.

Box 2.4. Development Assistance and the Successful Transition in Poland

Poland's transition performance has been excellent, both in comparison with other transition economies and in its own right. Poland was the first country to emerge from the transition recession, posting positive growth beginning in 1992. It has since maintained the highest average GDP growth rate of the non-post-conflict ECA transition economies, with growth averaging 3.7 percent from 1990 to 2001. In 1995, it became a member of OECD, and is today positioned for accession to the European Union.

As in other country cases surveyed in this paper, the impetus for reform came from Poland's government and people, and many partners were involved in providing support. Of these partners, the World Bank was an important player in the early phases of Poland's transition process, providing strong and effective advisory and financial support during the critical early stages of the economic transformation. The Bank was involved in all key areas of the systemic reform program: supporting Poland's reentry into the world economy through trade liberalization, stabilization of the economy, strengthening the currency and balance of payments, disposing of nonviable enterprises and restructuring those with a future, softening the negative impacts of reforms on vulnerable groups, creating the institutional and legal framework for a market economy, handing over control of the economy from the planners to the market, reducing the burden of controls and monopolies, encouraging the growth of private sector business, and mobilizing and coordinating other donor assistance. Bank analytical work, complemented by the dissemination activities of the Economic Development Institute (precursor of the World Bank Institute), was influential in fostering better understanding and acceptance of market-oriented policies in Poland.

The Bank was also an important contributor to reforms at the sectoral level. Bank support was significant in securing exceptional levels of debt reduction and in restoring Poland's creditworthiness. The Bank was also deeply involved in assisting to upgrade the country infrastructure in power, energy, transport, and telecommunications; in introducing new ideas, technology, and production methods; and in opening the door for private sector participation. Together with the IFC, the Bank helped to set up twinning arrangements that proved valuable in modernizing several Polish banks. In agriculture, the Bank's leadership helped to coordinate the efforts of various donors and gave reform in this sector a major impetus. Across sectors, the Bank's involvement helped put in place good management practices, transparent public procurement procedures, and strong environmental protection measures.

continued

Box 2.4. Development Assistance and the Successful Transition in Poland (continued)

One class of interventions that did not work very well during the early period was the support the Bank tried to provide for the restructuring of enterprises through credit lines. Polish banks were not equipped to handle them, and they were quickly surpassed by the development of domestic credit flows. These projects were cancelled, with substantial undisbursed balances, when they were clearly no longer necessary.

Poland deserves tremendous credit for being a front-runner in what was essentially new territory, and taking what were at the time regarded as huge risks, including making its currency convertible, lowering trade barriers, and hardening enterprise budgets while increasing competition. Nevertheless, while the overall record is overwhelmingly positive, Poland's growth has slowed sharply in the last two years. The country still faces a formidable agenda of reforms if it is to consolidate its major achievements of the past and benefit fully from EU accession. This agenda includes managing its fiscal deficit, restructuring public expenditure, reforming agriculture, completing the downsizing and restructuring of "old" industries, reinvigorating privatization, and completing reforms in health and education.

Such measures include combating crime, both organized and otherwise; dealing with corruption; implementing legal and judicial reform to ensure secure property rights, streamlined business licensing, and registration requirements; and building a tax system that encourages compliance rather than growth of a shadow economy. (Box 2.5 discusses governance challenges more generally, and the role of the World Bank in helping countries to address them over the past several years.)

Given the dangers described here, some of the early external policy advice appears, with hindsight, to have been simplistic: it concentrated too heavily on improving policies, and too little on building institutions. Furthermore, early expectations concerning the time it would take to complete the transition process turn out to have been highly optimistic. As a result of all these problems, it was not until after 1998 that the CIS countries as a group began to witness a recovery. (Recovery had started in many of the individual countries earlier.) As recovery has begun, however, these countries have grown more rapidly than Eastern Europe during the period 1999 through 2001.

Box 2.5. Helping Countries to Fight Corruption

Far from being the grease that oils an economy, corruption has a devastating economic and social impact. Corruption cripples development, threatens the rule of law, and challenges the institutional foundation for economic growth. Poor people are hit hardest, as they are most in need of services that protect physical safety and the security of assets and contracts, and provide health and education. They are least able to pay the cost of bribes and misappropriated public expenditure. World Bank research from Romania, for example, shows that low-income households are forced to spend more than 10 percent of their household income on bribes, compared with about 2 percent for high-income households. And corruption has a chilling effect on entrepreneurship, by similarly disadvantaging the small firms where poor people are most likely to work. Bank research in Ecuador and Peru finds that small firms pay 8 to 9 percent of their monthly revenue in bribes, compared with about 1 to 2 percent for large firms. (For an extensive bibliography of research findings on governance, corruption, and development, see Annex 5 of World Bank 2000d.) Corruption also undermines investor confidence, reduces aid effectiveness, and undermines both political and grassroots support for donor assistance. Ultimately it erodes the legitimacy of the state, in some cases resulting in a complete breakdown of law and order.

Until the mid-1990s, the Bank considered corruption as a political or sovereignty issue that was too sensitive to touch. Although the Bank has always safeguarded the integrity of its own operations and had started addressing the need for institutional strengthening in client countries by the mid-1980s, only a decade later did consensus grow around the view that corruption would have to be tackled explicitly by a development organization with poverty reduction as its central mandate. Nongovernmental organizations such as Transparency International (founded in 1993) helped to raise awareness of the problem, laying the groundwork for a shift in policy.

Leading this emerging consensus, the World Bank's President vowed in 1996, in his address at the Annual Meetings of the Bank and IMF, to fight the "cancer of corruption." Since then, the Bank has been committed to helping countries that request assistance in curbing corruption. The Bank does not seek to police corruption after the fact, but to work on the governance and public sector institutional reforms that can help inhibit it before it starts. The Bank's multi-pronged approach includes: increasing political accountability, strengthening civil society participation, creating a competitive private sector, ensuring restraints on power, and improving public sector management. At base, the Bank's assistance remains contingent on credible commitment by country authorities to that agenda.

continued

Box 2.5. Helping Countries to Fight Corruption (continued)

Since 1997 the Bank has learned and achieved much in this difficult area, and has expanded its partnerships with other organizations and donors. It has launched hundreds of lending, analytical, and capacity-building activities in over 95 countries. In Indonesia, for instance, impetus was provided by the upheavals of the last decade, which explicitly showed the dramatic and corrosive impact of corruption on economic and development achievements. Among other measures, the Bank is now supporting a multi-donor Indonesian-led Partnership for Governance Reforms to build a government, private sector, and civil society coalition for reform. In Guatemala, the Bank is building on long-standing programs of public sector institutional reform to support governance improvements, for example in public financial accountability. In Uganda, expenditure tracking surveys revealed that between 1991–1995, on average, less than 30 percent of nonwage expenditure allocations to schools were reaching their intended target, indicating massive leakage of funds. The government responded to this result by working on disbursement procedures and informing communities directly of disbursements. Receipts reported in the 2000 survey had risen to over 90 percent of disbursements.

2.4 Summary

We have learned much about the overall sources of growth and poverty reduction.

- Experience and analysis show that countries reduce poverty fastest when they put in place *two pillars of development:*

  - *create a good investment climate*—one that encourages firms, both small and large, to invest, create jobs, and increase productivity; and

  - *empower and invest in poor people*—by giving them access to health, education, social protection, and mechanisms for participating in the decisions that shape their lives.

- Understanding of *economic growth* and its causes has improved greatly. We now understand that sustained growth depends on broad progress in a number of areas: macroeconomic stability and trade openness; governance and institutions, including a good education system, effective legal institutions, and professional bureaucracy; vigorous competition; and adequate infrastructure, especially in countries that are landlocked or face other geographical barriers.

- **Poverty reduction** depends heavily on sustained economic growth. On average, income distribution does not worsen during periods of economic growth, so the incomes of poor people rise at the same rate as those of wealthier people. Countries that grew rapidly in the 1990s—such as China, India, Vietnam, and Uganda—managed to reduce the share of their people in absolute poverty by 5 to 8 percent per year.

- But while growth is essential, countries can accelerate reduction of income poverty by acting to ensure that poor people have the tools necessary to contribute to growth, such as health and education.

- Policies and investments aimed directly at reducing nonincome dimensions of poverty can be highly effective. Countries can accelerate health and education progress far beyond what would result simply from economic growth.

- Globally, we see this in the dramatic reductions in infant mortality, which has fallen steadily at each level of income as a result of improved technology, knowledge, and policies and institutions. The average country with $8,000 per capita income in 1950 would have had an infant mortality rate of 45 per 1,000 live births; by 1995, an average country at the same income level would have had an infant mortality rate of just 15 per 1,000 live births (a reduction of two-thirds).

Countries have acted on this knowledge by improving policies and institutions, often with very positive growth results.

- The development progress seen in many countries should be attributed primarily to actions by those countries themselves: specifically, improving the investment climate and investing in people.

- For example, macro stability and openness have improved throughout the developing world over the past two decades. The median inflation rate of developing countries was cut in half between 1982 and 1997, from about 15 to 7 percent. Average tariff rates have also declined sharply in all developing regions. In South Asia, for example, the unweighted average fell from about 65 percent in 1980–85 to 30 percent in 1996–98; in Latin American and the Caribbean, from 30 percent to under 15 percent.

- A group of countries that has integrated most quickly with the global economy—thanks to greater openness and improved investment climates—has grown very rapidly. This group of "rapid globalizers," which accounts for some 3 billion of the developing world's 5 billion people, saw per capita incomes increase by an astounding 5 percent per year in the 1990s. Even with fast-growing China excluded, the average was 3.5 percent.

However, development has been far from universal, and the roots of slow growth and decline can typically be traced to a bad climate for investment and productivity.

- The economic decline in much of Sub-Saharan Africa stems in part from a bad environment: large and persistent declines in the prices of exported commodities, high tariffs on exports, as well as adverse economic geography. But many African countries have compounded these and other historical disadvantages by failing to adopt good policies and institutions. Although policies have improved in recent years, governance and institutions remain a major problem in most SSA countries.

- Countries that have not grown rapidly—in Africa and elsewhere—have often failed to make progress on key features of the investment climate. For example, they may have achieved macro stability but not social stability; or they may have lowered trade barriers but not built the basic infrastructure necessary for international trade.

3. Cross-Country Evidence on the Effectiveness of Assistance

Chapters 1 and 2 have shown that rapid growth and development are possible, and that the development community has learned much about the policies and institutions needed for growth and poverty reduction—even if important gaps in our knowledge remain. Chapters 3 through 5 focus on how best to promote improvements in policies and institutions from outside. Have external actors, particularly the World Bank, been successful in helping to foster development? What broad lessons emerge about ways to enhance the effectiveness of aid?

Before analyzing the effects of development assistance, it is worthwhile to summarize the ways in which external agents can contribute to development. Development assistance encompasses both financial and nonfinancial instruments used in support of a country's own growth and poverty-reduction efforts. Resource transfer is an important part of development assistance, and the quantitative analysis in this section will focus largely on the effects of lending operations. But finance is only one of the instruments used to support development and, in some situations, it is not even the most useful one. Development assistance also includes analysis, advice, and capacity-building, either packaged with lending or on their own. Many of the country boxes in this paper highlight the importance of these nonlending tools, especially in environments—such as early in a reform era—when finance is not likely to contribute to poverty reduction. The mixture of instruments to be used in any particular country depends on the specifics of that country's needs and capacity.

As discussed in the Executive Summary, any attempt to assess the effectiveness of development assistance—and in particular of a single institution, such as the World Bank—confronts inherent analytical difficulties. The complexity of social and economic change means that the impact of aid cannot be separated easily from other factors. Because successful development requires country ownership, outside agents are unlikely to be the prime movers of development. Indeed, where they are central to the process, the sustainability of reform efforts may be in doubt. Even where external actors are clearly important, they will be most effective working in partnership with other external and internal partners, which makes it difficult to give credit or blame to any single institution. Finally, the need to "scale up"—to ensure that assistance is replicated or institutionalized, so that it has effects far beyond the boundaries of the specific intervention—means that even identifying the outcomes of a particular intervention is difficult.

To address these difficulties, we draw on as many types of evidence as possible. This section begins with the big-picture question of how to allocate and deliver large-scale financial assistance, drawing heavily on evidence from cross-country regressions. This type of analysis allows us to identify statistical correlations between aid flows and policy, on the one hand, and growth and poverty reduction on the other. Country cases (in boxes throughout this paper) and project evaluations (in chapters 4 and 5) complement the cross-country analysis by showing that results on the ground are consistent with the macro evidence.

3.1 Aid has a strongly positive effect on development—and this effect has grown in recent years, thanks to improved allocation and design.

At the economywide level, the evidence suggests strongly that aid promotes development, if the aid is provided under the right circumstances and with the right design. ODA in general has historically delivered substantial poverty reduction, and the poverty-reducing impact of ODA has increased in the past decade due to improved design and allocation. Empirical studies have shown that:

- **Well-targeted aid increases investment.** Each dollar of assistance provided through the Bank's concessional lending arm, the International Development Association (IDA), leads to nearly two dollars of additional private investment, including 60 cents of additional foreign direct investment. Thus aid draws in private investment, rather than crowding it out.

- **Well-targeted aid has high overall economic payoffs.** Because aid creates new economic possibilities, improving the investment climate and increasing investment, its economywide returns are far greater than even the direct poverty-reduction returns—with a rate of return as high as 40 percent in the case of IDA.

- **Aid has become far better targeted in recent years.** With the end of the Cold War, donors became less interested in using aid to achieve geopolitical goals and more interested in using aid for poverty reduction. Large-scale financial assistance is being increasingly allocated to countries that have reasonably good policies and institutions—that is, the countries that can best use aid for poverty reduction. With this shift, the poverty-reduction effectiveness of official development assistance (ODA) tripled during the 1990s.

The evidence on the effectiveness of aid has at times been ambiguous—but this is because early research failed to distinguish between different types of aid and recipients.

When all aid is lumped together, some analyses have found no clear relationship between aid and growth or poverty reduction.[51] But not all aid is aimed directly at poverty reduction, nor has aid always been provided in ways that will maximize growth. Moreover, because aid is often provided to help countries cope with external shocks, even if aid is reasonably well designed and allocated—and thus effective in helping the poor—the positive impact of such aid may be obscured by the magnitude of the shocks.

Disaster relief, for example, is not aimed directly at long-term poverty reduction and, thus, it is no surprise that such aid is not correlated with that result.[52] However, it does achieve its goal of helping to avert famine or assisting countries to recover from natural disasters. Similarly, large amounts of aid were directed at supporting the transition in Eastern Europe and Central Asia (ECA), for both political and economic reasons. There, the mandate in the early 1990s was explicitly to help transform these countries into market economies, rather than to focus directly on reducing poverty. More recently, as box 3.1 explains, the World Bank has played an important role in the international effort to promote peace and stability in the Balkans—a mission that is essential to poverty reduction, but not identical. Much aid during the Cold War was provided for military-oriented reasons, rather than developmental ones. In all of these cases, the lending—whether it is for transition or disaster relief or post-conflict stabilization—can help to build the foundations for poverty reduction, but the effects may appear only after a long lag. The end of the Cold War and the progress in transition have made possible a more direct targeting of aid to poverty reduction.

Beyond noting that aid with different goals has different results, research has also found that it is important to distinguish among the

Box 3.1. The World Bank in the Balkans: Development Assistance for Reconstruction and Stabilization

When the military conflict in Kosovo occurred in March 1999, the international community quickly recognized the potential economic dislocation for the region and the need for a coordinated response, not only in Kosovo but also in neighboring countries affected by the large influx of refugees, trade disruptions, and the collapse of investment. At that time, the G7 Finance Ministers requested that the World Bank and the European Commission lead the coordination effort of all bilateral and multilateral aid to the Balkans.

In response to this mandate, the World Bank played a key role in the reconstruction and development of South Eastern Europe, through:

- direct financial assistance—$600 million on average to the region, reaching $1 billion in the immediate aftermath of the Kosovo conflict;

- provision of advice on economic recovery and transition, institutional development, social policies, and design of regional development projects; and

- guidance of overall donor assistance, including assessment of financing needs and priorities for external financing.

The value of the Bank's contribution has been in its ability to deploy rapidly in response to change, developing in collaboration with its many partners a coherent view of economic and social development needs—beyond emergency and reconstruction—and thus facilitate the interventions of other donors:

- Based on the experience gained in other conflict-affected regions such as Bosnia and Herzegovina and the West Bank and Gaza, the Bank worked in Kosovo and more recently in Yugoslavia with many international and local organizations to build strong institutions and introduce market reforms, in order to ensure sustainable development beyond physical reconstruction.

continued

different environments in recipient countries. Aid to countries with relatively good policies and institutions has very different effects than aid to countries with worse policies and institutions. (The end of section 3.1 will address how best to assist the latter group of countries, given that large-scale aid is typically not effective in these environments.)

Box 3.1. The World Bank in the Balkans: Development Assistance for Reconstruction and Stabilization (continued)

- To support economic cooperation and integration, the World Bank worked in close partnership with the European Commission, the European Investment Bank (EIB), and the European Bank for Reconstruction and Development (EBRD) to develop a $2 billion Quick Start Package of regional projects and programs, and sectoral strategies and a financing mechanism for priority projects to implement these strategies.

- Following the change in government in Yugoslavia in October 2000, the World Bank provided policy advice and technical assistance for the development of the government's Economic Recovery and Transition Program, which outlined a comprehensive reform agenda, assessed financing needs and priorities, and provided the foundation for coordinating donor assistance to Yugoslavia.

It is difficult to assess the impact on the ground of the Bank's and its partners' many interventions, as only two and a half years have passed since the crisis. However, there are some early indications of what specific projects have achieved:

- The Kosovo Community Development Project benefited some 183,000 community members over the last two years through infrastructure microprojects in water supply, school rehabilitation, attention to sewage systems, and road building and maintenance, as well as social services projects and special training programs.

- To relieve Albania's immediate budgetary pressures from the massive inflow of refugees from Kosovo, the Bank processed and disbursed within 30 days a Public Expenditure Support Credit ($30 million).

- A post-conflict grant to FYR Macedonia ($2 million) addressed the needs of refugee children and youth and those of the hosting communities. The grant has reached 5,000 families through an Early Child Development network of mothers in disadvantaged communities inhabited by ethnic minorities or mixed groups. An additional 13,000 youth at risk have been reached through activities promoting social cohesion.

continued

Finally, the returns to aid will often be difficult to gauge because of the circumstances in which it is provided. Some developmentally successful countries, such as Korea in 1998, have received large aid inflows

---

Box 3.1. The World Bank in the Balkans: Development Assistance for Reconstruction and Stabilization (continued)

- An Emergency Economic Recovery Credit to FYR Macedonia ($15 million plus $25 million in cofinancing from the Netherlands, approved in December 2001) is helping to finance the budget on a noninflationary basis and to ease the foreign exchange constraint on the private sector at a critical time—after the crisis and while development aid had not yet resumed.

On a macro level, significant financial and technical resources have been mobilized in support of the region, regional cooperation has significantly improved, and the region as a whole has resumed growth:

- Over $6 billion of aid per year have been mobilized, on average, between 1999 and 2001 for the seven countries of the region.

- Intraregional trade has increased since 1999, not only in value but also as a share of total foreign trade, and a regionwide memorandum on free trade has been agreed.

- Growth in the region rebounded, from about 2 percent in 1999 to over 4 percent on average in 2001, with the exception of Macedonia.

Regional tensions have not been fully overcome, as evidenced especially by developments in Macedonia, but the coordinated regional program has helped to lessen those tensions.

---

during periods of economic setbacks—creating a misleading statistical correlation between aid and poor economic outcomes. Natural disasters will produce a similar correlation. In both cases, analysis of the proper counterfactual would often show that, relative to what would have happened otherwise, aid has contributed to better outcomes.

Research shows that ODA reduces poverty and spurs growth substantially when it goes to developing countries that have reasonably good policies and institutions.[53]

Experience and analysis have shown that it is generally not enough for donors simply to design projects well. In poor overall policy and institutional environments, the payoffs to flows of large-scale financial aid are on average very small. But where the environment is at least moderately good, then aid typically has large payoffs, as the remainder of this section will explain.[54]

Why would the overall environment matter so much in determining the effectiveness of ODA? The first reason is very straightforward: policies and institutions affect project quality. For example, a major reason for the dramatic decline in measured World Bank project outcomes in the 1970s and 1980s was the deterioration in policy quality and governance in many borrowing countries. No matter how well designed, a project can easily be undermined by high levels of macroeconomic volatility or of government corruption.

The second reason is more subtle. Even if a project does seem to succeed—based on narrow measures of economic returns and attainment of project objectives—the actual marginal contribution of aid funneled through that project may be small or even negative. This is because government resources are often largely fungible: money can be moved relatively easily from one intended use to another.[55] Thus if donors choose to finance a primary education project, displacing local money that would have been used for education, that local money could then be shifted to less productive purposes, such as military spending. In a country with poor public expenditure management, the displaced money could even be diverted to the personal uses of corrupt officials. In this case, the indirect but very real effect of aid could be to promote corruption.

Overall donor financial assistance is targeted far more effectively at poverty reduction than it was a decade ago.[56]

During the 1990s, overall aid allocation shifted in favor of countries with good policies. Aid is always driven by a variety of factors—poverty reduction goals among them, to be sure, but also geopolitical considerations, former colonial ties, human rights concerns, and other factors. During the Cold War, factors unrelated to poverty were especially important in driving aid allocations. This can be illustrated by both example and quantitative evidence:

- As an example, consider the case of Zaire under President Mobutu, which was clearly no one's ideal of a state dedicated to widespread poverty reduction. Policies were abysmal, and government officials diverted much aid money for their personal uses. Nevertheless, the international community allocated large amounts of aid to Zaire for reasons that were largely geopolitical. With its huge size and strategic location, Zaire was seen as a buffer against the spread of communism in southern and central Africa. Between 1960 and 2000, donors disbursed more than $10 billion in aid to Zaire, even as GNP per capita fell sharply through much of that period, from $460 in 1975 to $100 in 1996.

- Looking across countries, it is clear that the ability of the recipient country to use aid well was not a significant factor in total aid allocations as recently as 1990. Research using the World Bank's Country Policy and Instititional Assessments (CPIA) index of country environment has shown that in 1990 a large difference in the CPIA—that is, 1 additional point on a 6-point scale—corresponded to only a very small (and statistically insignificant) increase of about 8 percent in the per capita aid flows to the better-policy country.[57] Such a result is in keeping with the view that aid allocations up until this time were strongly influenced by factors other than the donor's desire to reduce poverty.

- Similarly, if we divide countries into three groups according to policy quality, we find that in 1990, countries with the best policies received an average of $39 per capita in overall aid, while those with the worst policies received more, at $44 per capita. Even in the case of a single country, aid levels often failed to rise as policies improved, or fall as policies deteriorated. In Zambia, for example, aid levels rose as policy deteriorated in the 1970s and 1980s.[58]

- Because the World Bank was less constrained than bilateral donors by geopolitical objectives, IDA was already relatively well targeted in terms of poverty reduction in 1990, and has since improved further. The same holds for the Bank's nonconcessional lending through IBRD, the allocation of which is strongly influenced by the Bank's assessment of countries' policies and institutions.

Since the end of the Cold War, and increasingly through the 1990s, donor countries and other aid agencies have reallocated assistance in ways that strengthened poverty reduction.

- By 1997–98, good-policy countries received $28 per capita, in net disbursements, or almost twice as much as the poor-policy countries ($16.4 per capita).

- How much has this shift increased the efficiency of poverty reduction? One set of estimates suggests that in 1990, another $1 billion in net disbursements allocated proportionately to ODA would have lifted an estimated 105,000 people permanently out of poverty. But with the improved 1997–98 allocations, an additional one-time expenditure of $1 billion in ODA would have lifted an estimated 284,000 people permanently out of poverty. While these estimates are merely indicative, they suggest that *the poverty-reduction productivity of ODA nearly tripled during the 1990s.*[59]

It was not only waning geopolitical concerns, but also a more extensive knowledge base and greater transparency that contributed to this shift. Research into aid effectiveness undermined both polar positions about aid: that aid was always effective or that aid was never effective. This knowledge helped to focus attention on the key question of whether the right countries were receiving aid. The continuing challenge is to keep development aid focused on poverty reduction and to improve its effectiveness.

Despite the improvement in aid targeting and effectiveness, donor countries have not responded with an increase in ODA flows; in fact, those flows decreased during the past decade.

Aid flows dropped substantially over the 1990s in real terms, and by 2000 stood at about 7 percent less than the 1990 level. With the growth in incomes in the rich countries over that period, aid levels expressed as a share of donors' GNP fell even more sharply—from 0.33 percent in 1990 to 0.22 percent in 2000. By the end of this period, aid accounted for less than 1 percent of donor countries' total government expenditure.[60]

World Bank assistance has on average been well targeted at poverty reduction.

Like other types of ODA, IDA was affected by pressures to lend to countries for reasons not directly connected with poverty reduction, particularly during the Cold War. Nevertheless, the evidence suggests that IDA lending was less affected than overall ODA. We can see this in the statistics on the relationship between poverty, policy, and IDA. Even in 1990, more IDA went to the good-policy countries ($4.7 per capita) than to the poor-policy countries ($2 per capita). And IDA was already more than four times as responsive to policy improvements than ODA was (in that a 1-point improvement in policy on the Bank's rating scale led to a 36 percent increase in aid per capita).

By 1997–98, IDA allocation had improved substantially even from this good base. Good policy countries now received $6.5 per capita, compared with $2.3 per capita in poor-policy countries. Or, to express it in terms of marginal efficiency of poverty reduction, an additional $1 billion allocated like average IDA would lift an estimated 434,000 people out of poverty. This means that *IDA is about 60 percent more efficient than it was in 1990, and 50 percent more efficient than overall ODA.*[61]

High IDA repayment rates are also consistent with the view that the aid is going to countries that typically are able to make good use of it.

- IDA repayment rates are very high. As table 3.1 shows, only about 5 percent of expected IDA repayments were in nonaccrual status in 2000 and 2001; uncollected payments were concentrated in a handful of states, many of them mired in extended conflict.[62] Given the evidence that IDA is well targeted at countries that are serious about growth and poverty reduction, this should not be so surprising. Countries that put in place reasonable policies and institutions generally earn enough of a return on aid that they can afford to make repayments.[63]

- A substantial share (39 percent) of IDA reflows come either from countries that have graduated entirely from IDA (11 percent) or from "blend" countries that receive both nonconcessional IBRD lending and IDA lending (28 percent).

- Debt relief for the HIPC countries does not substantially change this picture, for two reasons. First, HIPC represents a recognition that a country's debt service payments are not sustainable in a manner consistent with development; however, those unsustainable debts are not primarily IDA. Second, total estimated HIPC debt relief represents only a small share of the total outstanding IDA portfolio—about 13 percent of total credits outstanding.

Table 3.1. IDA Overdue Payments, 1992–2001

Fiscal year	1992	1993	1994	1995	1996	1997	1998	1999	2000	2001
Amount (US$ million)	6	15	49	43	50	57	49	102	95	82
As share of expected repayments (percent)	1	2	6	4	5	5	4	6	5	5

Nonconcessional lending (IBRD) also goes primarily to countries with good ratings for policies and institutions. It does not typically go to countries with the highest ratings, for reasons noted above: these countries tend to have good, if volatile, access to capital markets and may not borrow from IBRD during periods of good access. Over the past five years (FY1996–2001), about 40 percent of all IBRD-eligible countries received good ratings (not including countries with the highest ratings), but these borrowers accounted for more than two-thirds of all new lending commitments.

Well-targeted aid not only reduces poverty, but also has far wider effects. Aid crowds in private investment, both domestic and foreign, by improving the investment climate.

Well-designed aid crowds in private investment, both domestic and foreign. Aid is not simply a transfer payment for the consumption of poor people, but an investment in improved policies and institutions. The best aid finances the costs of change, rather than the costs of not changing.

As a result, the investment climate improves when aid is well designed and well allocated. Research shows that *IDA flows on average lead to increases in gross investment nearly twice as large as the value of the aid itself.* In good policy environments, in both low- and middle-income countries, *aid also increases foreign direct investment substantially—by 60 cents for each dollar of aid.*[64]

Aid spurs economywide growth, benefiting people of all income groups; and as a result, it has very high overall returns.

The crowding-in effect on investment means that the returns to aid are far higher than the poverty-reduction effects alone would suggest. Indeed, it has been estimated that *the overall average return to IDA may be as high as 40 percent.*[65]

China is an excellent example of a country in which aid investments in support of a country-owned development strategy helped to improve the investment climate and encourage rapid private-sector-led growth and poverty reduction (box 3.2). But the crowding-in effects of aid extend also to smaller countries whose reforms are less

Box 3.2. World Bank Assistance and Reform in China

China was a low-income country when it began its market-oriented reforms in the late 1970s, after 30 years of attempts at various forms of a planned economy. The World Bank's interaction with China had a significant impact in sustaining the reform momentum, as confirmed by independent analysis. It provided top Chinese policymakers with the first in-depth overall economic analysis of China's development problems, as well as studies of key sectors in the 1980s. The Bank helped to increase the confidence and persistence of reformers, recommended some specific policies and institutions, and trained government officials in "market economy" skills (from project financing to international procurement). Bank assistance was instrumental in helping the Chinese economy engage with the outside world, both through advice on trade liberalization and exchange-rate unification, and through helping modernize Chinese ports. In short, at a time when the government was very suspicious of the outside world, the World Bank was a trusted advisor and helped lay the foundation for the private investment that has underpinned China's success.

The result of China's reform has been the greatest poverty reduction in history, with much of the reduction in absolute poverty taking place in rural areas. The sharp fall in rural poverty (from 34 percent of the population in 1985 to 18 percent in 1998) benefited from about 65 Bank-assisted rural development projects and associated sector work, including studies aimed specifically at identifying and addressing the changing causes of acute rural poverty. Bank partnership with China in the social sectors, most notably in a series of large-scale basic education and health projects, contributed to the steady progress made in human capital development and the striking improvements in development indicators. Bank policy advice and financial support similarly assisted China to put in place the physical infrastructure and related sectoral policies critical to national growth, particularly construction of the transport system that facilitated market integration, and energy policies increasingly shaped by bold reform goals. Finally, the past decade saw major progress in the Bank's assistance to China in formulating and pursuing a much-strengthened national environmental agenda.

In the whole range of this work—and China is the Bank's largest client for both policy advice and investment support—the Chinese government has shown strong commitment to the Bank. A key indicator of that commitment is the strength of the China project portfolio, which has for years been one of the Bank's best-performing portfolios.

well known to investors. In Mauritania, for example, aid-supported reform of telecommunications has prompted a surge of investments and economic activity (box 3.3).

These strong and improving effects of aid have come despite major challenges to development effectiveness, such as the problem of crippling debt. Excessive lending (including by official agencies), unfavorable shocks, and weak policies led to unsustainable levels of debt in many low-income countries, with the debt overhang contributing to poverty traps. The HIPC debt relief initiative has attempted to reduce this barrier to development.

Box 3.3. Making Competition Work in Infrastructure: Telecommunications Reform in Mauritania

In mid-1998, Mauritania faced several constraints as it embarked on a program of competitive and private provision of infrastructure services: relatively high country risk, a small domestic market, and a virtual absence of institutional capacity for regulating competitive utility sectors. By the end of 2001, Bank-supported reforms in telecommunications had largely overcome these constraints, laying the foundations for similar reforms in other utility sectors such as power and water. The monopoly of the state-owned telecommunications operator ended in mid-2000 when the first mobile telecommunications license was granted through a competitive tender; the tender generated proceeds of $US28 million, a record among emerging market economies. Eight months later, in February 2001, a competitive tender for privatizing the state-owned operator yielded a postprivatization enterprise value of $4,065 per access line, well above the previous record for Sub-Saharan Africa as well as the world average of $2,500. Competing in all segments of telecommunications services, both operators have now multiplied access lines from 20,000 at the beginning of 2000 to over 130,000 by end-2001. Furthermore, competition has accelerated investment in the sector, which in just two years (2000 and 2001) totaled more than 10 percent of GDP.

A windfall from competition has been the creation of 2,000 telecommunications-related jobs in the informal sector, as over 300 microenteprises have sprung up in the main cities to sell prepaid calling cards and mobile handsets and repair telephone equipment. Similar reforms in the power sector have benefited from a significantly improved country risk as well as a well-tested institutional framework for privatization and for regulation.

During the commodity price boom of the 1970s, many poor developing countries responded by increasing domestic expenditures. These expenditures were amplified through increases in external borrowing, including from multilateral, bilateral, and commercial sources. Both the borrowing countries and the lenders believed incorrectly that high commodity prices and export earnings would be long-lived.

When an oil-price shock and global recession hit in the late 1970s and early 1980s, the borrowing countries suddenly faced a debt service crunch. Commodity prices turned sharply against the non-oil commodity exporters, making it difficult to pay for both imports and debt service. Official lending increased to help cushion the effects of the shock, and to substitute for finance from commercial sources, which soon evaporated. Official lending and grants then continued as support for adjustment of policies to the new environment.

But in many of the highly indebted countries, the expected improvements in policy performance did not materialize, whether because of insufficient commitment by borrowers or because the design of the adjustment had not paid enough attention to social concerns. (Section 3.2 discusses the problems of spurring growth when borrowing countries are not sufficiently committed to reform.) In other cases, reforms did not lead to the expected supply and growth response. As a result, the GDP average growth rate between 1980 and 1987 of the 33 countries that were characterized in the mid-1990s as the most severely indebted low-income countries was just 1.9 percent—which translated into an income decline in per capita terms. The cumulative effect of the shock and economic decline was that a debt burden that had been very reasonable quickly became unsustainable. Between 1982 and 1992, the debt-to-export ratio of these 33 countries rose from 266 to 620 percent.[66]

The international community has attempted to address the problem through a variety of debt-reduction mechanisms since the late 1980s. In 1996, it went a step further, creating the Highly Indebted Poor Countries (HIPC) debt relief initiative. Box 3.4 describes briefly the design and achievements of this initiative.

It is important to note that, although official lending contributed to debt accumulation in these countries and debt reductions through HIPC have generally been substantial, problem lending was only a small portion of total IDA lending. Most of the population of the low-income world is in countries that have been able to keep their debts at

---

Box 3.4. The Highly Indebted Poor Countries (HIPC) Debt Relief Initiative

Efforts to deepen debt relief for poor countries suffering from unsustainable debt burdens culminated in the Highly Indebted Poor Countries (HIPC) Initiative, launched in 1996. This initiative aims to increase the effectiveness of aid by helping poor countries achieve sustainable levels of debt while strengthening the link between debt relief and strong policy performance. Forty-two countries, primarily from the Sub-Saharan Africa region, are identified as eligible to receive debt relief under this initiative. In 1999 the scope of the initiative was widened to accelerate and deepen the provision of debt relief. As of December 2001, 24 countries have reached the decision point (the point where debt relief is approved by the Executive Boards of the IMF and the World Bank and interim relief begins). These countries are now receiving debt service relief that will amount to about $36 billion over time, with a $21 billion reduction in the present value of their outstanding debt stock.

For the 24 countries that have reached their decision points, HIPC alone has reduced the present value of external debt by about half. When combined with other debt reduction mechanisms, this implies a two-thirds reduction in these countries' external indebtedness.

Not only does HIPC reduce debt overhang, but it also supports positive change toward better poverty reduction. Debt relief under the HIPC Initiative is intended for countries that are pursuing effective poverty reduction strategies, and both better public expenditure management and increased social expenditures are critical elements of this. For the countries that have reached decision points under the HIPC Initiative, the ratio of social expenditures to GDP is projected to increase from 5.8 to 6.9 percent between 1998–99 and 2001–03. The challenge is to ensure that these expenditures translate into better social-sector outcomes and, more importantly, that the broader policy environment continues to improve and support growth and poverty reduction.

---

sustainable levels; as a result, the estimated total IDA debt forgiveness under HIPC amounts to about 13 percent of the portfolio.

The development community now recognizes that large-scale financial assistance has little effect on poverty reduction in countries with weak institutions, policies, and governance. The World Bank is working to increase its knowledge and effectiveness in this important and difficult area.

Box 3.5. Mozambique: From Civil War to Rapid Growth

Mozambique over the last decade has emerged as an example of successful reform, one that is perhaps less well known than others discussed in this paper. The country emerged in 1992 from a long civil war, which—together with bearing the costs of its frontline status in isolating the apartheid government in South Africa—had left the country one of the poorest in the world. GDP per capita in 1992 was only $133.

In the years following the end of the war, the World Bank helped the government to design and implement key measures in financial liberalization, exchange rate reform, trade liberalization, and privatization through a series of adjustment operations. The ensuring recovery has been impressive:

- After growing just 0.1 percent on average over the previous decade, GDP grew at an average of 8.4 percent annually from 1993 through 2001.

- Inflation, which had averaged 53.3 percent annually between 1993 and 1996, fell to an average of 3.3 percent in 1997–99.

- Social indicators also improved in this better environment: the gross primary admission rate rose from 57 percent in 1995 to over 100 percent in 2000, while the repetition rate fell somewhat from 26 percent in 1995 to 23 percent in 2000.

- Private investment, crowded in by the better policies, helped to spur this growth. For example, direct foreign investment grew some 500 percent between 1992 and 2001.

- Export growth improved dramatically, from –6.8 percent (1980–90) to 15.1 percent (1990–2000)

- Agricultural growth was revitalized, accelerating from 1.3 percent annually (1985–92) to 9.8 percent annually (1993–2001).

Other intermediate indicators show progress toward a better environment for growth and poverty reduction. Government transparency and accountability have increased: a Medium Term Expenditure Framework was introduced in 1999, and publication of quarterly budget execution reports started in 2000. Furthermore, more resources are being allocated to the social sectors: under HIPC, combined current expenditures on health and education increased by $60 million in the two years prior to 2000, accounting for more than 80 percent of the total increase in current spending over the period.

continued

Box 3.5. Mozambique: From Civil War to Rapid Growth (continued)

Not everything has gone well. Two banks that were partially privatized in the mid-1990s experienced problems owing in part to a lack of internal controls, requiring reprivatization and recapitalization. And Mozambique still faces very serious development challenges: a countrywide HIV prevalence rate of some 12 percent; a judicial and legal system in need of reform; and a tax system that yields revenues of only 12 percent of GDP, well below the average for the region. Nevertheless, the progress over 10 years has laid a good foundation for tackling these and other development problems.

While aid effectiveness requires that large-scale financial assistance be allocated to poor countries that have demonstrated the capacity to use aid well, the international community cannot simply abandon people who live in countries that lack the policies, institutions, and governance necessary for sustained growth and for effective use of aid. Poor people in these countries are among the poorest in the world and face the greatest hurdles in improving their lives. Experience suggests that current technical assistance for capacity-building efforts, as well as the promise of greater financial assistance if policies, institutions, and governance improve, are often insufficient to enable these countries to initiate and sustain reform. A World Bank task force is now exploring new approaches for helping people and fostering change in these countries, which are sometimes known as Low Income Countries under Stress (LICUS).

Of the two or three dozen countries with the poorest institutions and policies, only a few have made major improvements in the environments for growth and poverty reduction over the past decade, in contrast to the broad improvements in policies in other developing countries. Ethiopia, Mozambique, and Uganda are unusual among former LICUS countries in having achieved significant progress.[67] (See box 3.5 for a discussion of the role of Bank assistance in Mozambique.) Other LICUS countries have seen little development progress, and the performance of the Bank lending portfolio in this group has been poor: projects have failed at double the rate for other countries.

Approaches that work in the typical low-income country may not be appropriate in the LICUS, as they typically lack the basis for county leadership of reform, and traditional lending conditionality has not worked well in inducing and supporting reform. Given the weaknesses in governance and central institutions, there may at times be a role for the development community to become more directly involved in the provision of basic health and education services.

These countries vary widely in their problems and opportunities. As is the case for the better-performing countries, no single strategy will be appropriate for all of the LICUS; each country has its specific challenges and must look to its unique solutions. Nevertheless, it is useful to distinguish approaches in LICUS countries from those that will work in countries with better policies, institutions, and governance.

- *Large-scale financial transfers are unlikely to work well, because the absorptive capacity in these environments is quite limited.*

- *Instead, donors should focus on knowledge transfer and capacity-building to facilitate change.* Given the constraints on government capacity, such efforts should concentrate on a limited reform agenda that is both sensible in economic terms (that is, mindful of sequencing issues) and feasible from a sociopolitical standpoint. Only when they develop greater capacity will these countries generally be able to make good use of large-scale aid.

- *In the LICUS, there will often be a case for using aid to improve basic health and education services.* To be effective, however, funding should probably be directed through channels other than the central government. The LICUS task force suggests wholesale-retail structures in which a donor-monitored wholesaling organization contracts with multiple channels of retail provision, such as the private sector, NGOs, and local governments.

Another related challenge has been to provide the necessary support for Sub-Saharan Africa, and to overcome the legacy of poor policies and institutions, sometimes compounded by donor mistakes.

Africa has unfortunately been the region in which most of the development failures discussed elsewhere in this paper have converged, deepening the poverty of the region's people. Chapter 2 noted that country environments in much of Africa have been characterized by poor governance and weak institutions, so that even as policies improved, these factors often served as brakes on development. But problems with the design and delivery of aid also had an effect. Especially during the Cold War, political factors drove much of the aid allocation to the region, which meant that donors often impeded change and reform rather than supporting it.[68] Adjustment lending suffered from weak ownership, and even where there was local commitment, local capacity was sometimes overwhelmed by the complexity of project design. Furthermore, both international lenders and African borrowers believed incorrectly in the early 1980s that the decline in commodity prices was a temporary phenomenon; this belief led to unsustainable levels of borrowing.

Improvements in policies and institutions in many Sub-Saharan African countries, combined with examples of successful poverty reduction in a few countries, now provide grounds for hope. As policies improved, so did economic performance: GDP growth rates rose to an average of 4.3 percent in 1994–98, or nearly 2 percentage points higher than in the 1980s.[69] And a few countries, such as Uganda and Mozambique, have seen especially strong returns to reform. These developments have important implications for aid allocation: although not every country in Africa could absorb an increase in large-scale aid (for reasons described in the previous section), as the returns to aid rise, so too should the amount of aid allocated to the region. Instead, African countries with good policy saw a substantial decline in aid flows in the 1990s, with aid per capita falling by roughly a third, even as prices for export commodities also fell sharply.

3.2 In the right environments and with the right design, adjustment (or policy-based) lending has been broadly effective in spurring growth.

Laying the foundations for growth typically requires considerable structural reform of the economy. To support this process, the Bretton Woods institutions have provided structural adjustment loans for the past two decades. Adjustment lending is intended to help member countries design and implement reform programs that contribute to the creation of economic conditions that are conducive to economic growth. Adjustment lending grew out of the recognition that, as discussed in Section 3.1, the overall policy and institutional environment heavily influences the success rate of projects; and that with the oil shocks of the 1970s, the overall environment had become far less favorable to development.[70] With experience, the Bank has learned to better take into account the potential distributive impacts of some aspects of structural adjustment programs. The Bank now works with borrowers to strengthen social protection mechanisms in order to ensure that poor people do not bear an unfair share of the short-term adjustment costs.

Adjustment can contribute, and often has contributed, to growth and poverty reduction.

In assessing the effectiveness of adjustment lending in spurring growth and poverty reduction, it is important to look separately at the impact of adjustment on growth and poverty reduction and the link between adjustment lending and the design and implementation of adjustment programs.

Some observers have questioned the existence of a systematic link in developing countries between significant economic reforms—or structural adjustment—and economic growth and poverty reduction.[71] However, as noted above, there is strong evidence of a clear and robust link between improving economic policies and growth, and between growth and poverty reduction.[72] First, economic growth in developing countries on average increases the income of poor people proportionally: that is, as noted earlier, a 1-percent increase in per-capita GDP tends on average to lead to a 1-percent increase in the incomes of the poorest quintile of the population. (It is important to stress that this is only an average, and that specific countries, regions, or groups may be left behind; adjustment design and implementation need to anticipate and respond to this variation in outcomes.)

Second, cross-country evidence shows that successfully implemented adjustment policies have tended to increase growth rates on average with little effect on income distribution. Policies such as trade openness, low inflation, moderate size of government, and strong rule of law have generally benefited the incomes of poor people as much as those of anyone else. Indeed, stabilization of high inflation has tended to benefit the poor more than others. Furthermore, since adjustment programs are often launched in times of economic crisis, their effect on growth and poverty reduction tends to be underestimated in cross-country analyses. Research simulating the effect of not adjusting as a counterfactual suggests that adjustment experiences were both better for economic growth and more equitable than not adjusting.[73]

Generally, these findings support the view that structural adjustment can be a powerful instrument for growth and poverty reduction, but it is equally clear that in specific country experiences the distributional impacts can be quite different from the average. This suggests the need for carefully analyzing the poverty impact of adjustment policies under local conditions, to ensure that we can support an adjustment with positive effects on poor people.

The performance of adjustment operations has been mixed, especially during the 1980s, as a result of insufficient country ownership and insufficient attention to social dimensions.

Adjustment lending helps countries to undertake reforms and smooth the transition costs associated with adjusting to economic shocks—but only if critical reforms are actually carried out. The record of World Bank adjustment lending is mixed in this regard;[74] it includes both a number of success stories and a number of cases where adjustment lending was not followed by reform implementation.[75]

Bank reviews and studies concluded from the experience of the 1980s that country commitment is one of the most critical conditions for ensuring the success of reforms supported by adjustment lending.[76] Evidence has shown that policy change is driven by the country's own initiative, capacity, and political readiness, rather than by foreign assistance and associated loan conditionality.[77] Heavy reliance on conditionality is ineffective for several reasons: it can be difficult to monitor whether a government has in fact fulfilled the conditions, particularly when external shocks muddy the picture; governments may revert to old practices as soon as the money has been disbursed; and when assessments are subjective, donors may have an incentive to emphasize progress in order to keep programs moving. *Without country ownership, adjustment lending has not only failed to support reforms, but has probably contributed to their delay. For example, case studies of Côte d'Ivoire, the Democratic Republic of Congo, Kenya, Nigeria, and Tanzania all concluded that the availability of aid money in the 1980s postponed much-needed reforms.*[78]

In practice, country commitment has often proved difficult to assess. For example, a government may be seriously committed to a reform program but subsequently find it impossible to implement key measures, sometimes for reasons not fully under the government's control. In other cases, the government may be interested primarily in the funds, not in the reforms on which the funding is conditional. For this reason, the government's track record—measured by the quality of the policies and institutions it has already put in place—is often a good indicator of its commitment to reform. Research has shown that in good policy and institutional environments, well-designed adjustment lending succeeds in accelerating, broadening, and deepening reforms and in enhancing their impact on growth and poverty reduction.[79]

Early adjustment operations also sometimes suffered from insufficient attention to the social dimensions of adjustment. As noted above, the evidence suggests that on balance poor people benefit from adjustment and reform as much as other groups.[80] Nevertheless, even successful, market-friendly reforms have benefits and costs that are distributed unevenly, especially in the near term, and design and implementation of adjustment operations need to take this factor into account.

The World Bank has applied these lessons through better targeting of adjust-ment loans and more selective use of conditionality.

The Bank has increasingly focused adjustment lending on borrowers with a satisfactory track record. At the same time, the Bank also supports reforms in countries where improvements in the policy environment suggest the potential for a turnaround. Judging from CPIA ratings, the strength of the link between IDA disbursements and country policy performance tripled between FY1990 and FY1997–98. The increasing performance-based selectivity in World Bank (IDA and IBRD) lending decisions also shows up in the share of adjustment loans to countries with above-average performance on a broad range of policies, again according to CPIA ratings. In FY1995–2000 that share amounted to 72 percent.

Increased country selectivity—due to learning and the post-Cold War decline in geopolitically motivated lending—led to dramatic increases in the development effectiveness of adjustment lending, as evaluated by the independent Operations Evaluation Department (OED).[81] OED's outcome ratings typically measure to what extent an operation has achieved its objectives and thus provide a good indica-tor for the strength of the link between adjustment lending and the implementation of the program being supported by the loans. The share of operations rated satisfactory in outcome increased from 68 percent in FY1990–94 to 86 percent in FY1999–2000.[82] In terms of lending volumes, the increase was even more pronounced, from 73 percent in FY1990–94 to 97 percent in FY1999–2000. OED ratings of long-term sustainability (an assessment of resilience to risk) and of institutional development (the contribution of operations to capacity building) also increased over the same period. The share of satisfactory ratings of sustainability increased from 62 to 81 percent, and that of satisfactory ratings of institutional development increased from 44 to 71 percent (both percentages refer to the share of lending in dollar terms).

Stronger borrower ownership has contributed to more successful adjustment.

As noted above, experience with adjustment lending has been mixed, although the quality of such lending has improved over time. Adjustment lending was most successful when there was strong government involvement in the design of the program, the country had relatively good institutions, and the program extended beyond the confines of a specific Bank operation.

A good example of the latter condition is Mexico's rural sector. In the late 1980s and early 1990s, the Bank was involved in two agricultural adjustment loans that supported privatization and price liberalization. However, some of the most important aspects of the government's adjustment program were not financially supported by Bank lending. Rather, they came about as a result of the dialogue and analysis that were initiated with adjustment loans (such as the land reform of the *ejido* sector, as well as the trade and price liberalization of their major crops, maize and beans).[83]

This Mexico example is not unique. Other developing countries such as Vietnam (see box 3.6) have also had strong country ownership of their reforms, and have charted their own course while making good use of international assistance (both knowledge-based and financial). But other countries have borrowed without fully accepting the conditions placed on the loans, and both reform design and implementation have suffered as a result.

**Box 3.6. Vietnam and the World Bank: Learning
before Lending**

Vietnam has moved strongly to reform its economy and reduce poverty
over the past dozen years, beginning when it was still politically and economically estranged from major donors and therefore unable to receive
large-scale aid. The Bank began cautiously to provide advice to Vietnam
in 1989, at a time when the country's disastrous economic policies had
produced a crisis of hyperinflation, falling economic activity, and mass
exodus of economic migrants. Although it did not provide finance until
1993, the Bank advised the government on stabilizing the macroeconomy,
opening to foreign trade and investment, and reforming property rights
(through return of land to household farmers and introduction of laws for
private companies and foreign direct investment).

Vietnam saw strong results from its initial reforms, and by 1993 the economy was growing rapidly in the reformed environment. At that point,
infrastructure problems (ports, roads, and power) became serious bottlenecks. The Bank then began to finance projects that combined infrastructure development with policy reform to encourage private-sector
participation. The Bank also helped with reform and expansion of the
primary education system, which has helped ensure broad participation
in Vietnam's growth and development. Bank-designed household surveys
in 1992 and 1998 demonstrate the effectiveness of reform: the poverty
rate was cut from 58 to 37 percent in just six years.

Dramatic poverty reduction in Vietnam—as in China, India, Uganda, and
other countries highlighted here—did not depend on getting everything
right. All of these countries continue to face major development challenges, and suffer from gaps in areas of policies, institutions, and governance; none has achieved a perfectly functioning market economy. Their
success shows that the returns to moving in the right direction can be
very strong, and that development assistance can help (and has helped)
countries to make that progress.

**3.3 Donors and recipient countries have worked to make aid more
effective through the PRSP process, which stresses greater country
ownership and a poverty outcomes approach.**

The lesson that strong borrower ownership is essential for economywide reform, together with the need for improved coordination among
donors and greater attention to poverty goals, led the World Bank, the

International Monetary Fund, and their partners to adopt a new framework for development assistance organized around the recipient's preparation of a Poverty Reduction Strategy Paper (PRSP).

The PRSP approach

In December 1999, the Boards of the IMF and the World Bank approved a new approach to the challenge of reducing poverty in low-income (IDA) countries, based on country-owned poverty reduction strategies that would serve as a framework for development assistance. As of December 2001, 41 countries had prepared Interim-PRSPs (I-PRSPs), and 10 countries had completed full PRSPs. The underlying goals of the PRSP process (reflecting the principles of the Comprehensive Development Framework) are to ensure broad-based country ownership of poverty reduction strategies; develop strategies that take a comprehensive, long-term perspective; focus on results that matter for the poor; and to build stronger partnerships between low-income countries and the international donor community.

Early results of the PRSP approach

After two years of implementation of the PRSP initiative, the IMF, the Bank, the PRSP teams and partners collected their experience in order to learn how to implement PRSPs most effectively. The PRSP approach, with its emphasis on country ownership and flexibility, challenges the multilaterals to change their way of working. The current review of the PRSP process reveals that there seems to be widespread agreement (among national PRSP teams, donors, and civil society organizations) on five key achievements:

- There is a strong sense of commitment among most governments of their poverty reduction strategies.

- The participatory processes have created a more open dialogue within governments and with at least some parts of civil society than had previously existed.

- Issues related to poverty reduction, including issues of governance and corruption, have taken a more prominent place in national policy making and expenditures (see bullet below).

- The need to base a poverty strategy on a comprehensive assessment of the poverty in each country has provided a substantial impetus to the poverty information and knowledge base.

- The donor community as a whole has embraced the principles of the PRSP approach, providing technical and financial support to countries in PRSP preparation and indicating their intention to align their assistance programs to support PRSPs.[84]

Recent IMF staff analysis has compared budget allocations from 1999 (pre-PRSP) with the projected expenditure levels for 2001–02 for 32 low-income countries with active PRSP programs. The results clearly indicate that full PRSPs are associated with an increased emphasis on "pro-poor spending."[85] For the first group of seven countries with full PRSPs, the increase in "poverty-reducing" spending is about 20 percent larger from 1999 to 2000–01 than for the other PRSP countries analyzed. Overall increases in such spending for the full PRSP countries, relative to 1999, has been substantial, on the order of 30 percent of the budget as a share of GDP (that is, poverty-reducing spending is projected to rise from 7.7 to 10.2 percent of GDP between 1999 (pre-PRSP) and 2001–02). While these results are encouraging, this is obviously a narrow measure of success. It is important to bear in mind that these budgetary reallocations will translate into improved poverty outcomes only if there are corresponding improvements in budget execution, service delivery, and access for the poor, and in the investment climate. It is in large measure the investment climate that will determine whether there are job opportunities to match the growth in human capital.

Participants in the PRSP review also identified areas for improvement. They noted that the task of developing a strategy that deals comprehensively with macroeconomic policy, structural and sectoral reforms, governance issues, social inclusion, and the medium-term public expenditure program is extremely complex. Targets set by countries are often overly ambitious. Policy changes and programs to reach them should be better prioritized, so as to ensure realism and to facilitate effective implementation. Setting clearer priorities will require better understanding of the impact of policy actions on the poor, improved public expenditure management systems, and a greater investment in monitoring poverty outcomes. Another challenge concerns the human development sectors, such as health and education; a recent review suggested that these sectors (including their budgetary implications) were not fully integrated with the rest of the PRSP.

Finally, the interaction among the principles of country ownership, partnerships, and results orientation also gives rise to an issue that bears special mention: the potential tension between the principle of country ownership and the need for donors to be accountable for the effective use of their resources. Inevitably, there will be some divergence in donor and country views about the right policies and about capacities for implementation. Donors are being called on to align their assistance programs to support in a coordinated manner some, if not all, aspects of countries' PRSPs, within the institutional and capacity constraints that each donor faces. Donors—including the World Bank—as part of their contribution need to apply the lessons on pro-poor growth and to support countries to undertake the necessary reforms. This is likely to be a permanent part of development assistance, and addressing it is part of the job of donors. With the PRSP process, this is beginning to happen.

3.4 Summary

Macro-level evidence shows that development assistance has generally accelerated growth and poverty reduction, and that its poverty-reduction impact has increased over time.

- Both statistical evidence and country-level case studies demonstrate that large-scale financial aid can generally be used effectively for poverty reduction, where reasonably good policies are in place.

- By this criterion, donor financial assistance is targeted far more effectively at poverty reduction than it was a decade ago when Cold War geopolitics still heavily influenced aid allocations.

- In 1990, countries with bad policies received $44 per capita, while those with good policies (as defined by the World Bank's policy and institutional performance rating system) received less: only $39 per capita. By the late 1990s, the situation was reversed: good-policy countries received $28 per capita, or almost twice as much as the poor-policy countries ($16 per capita).

- As a result, the poverty-reduction effectiveness of each dollar of official development assistance (ODA) has grown rapidly. It is estimated that in 1990, another $1 billion allocated proportionately to ODA would have lifted some 105,000 people permanently out of poverty; by 1997–98, that number had improved to an estimated 284,000 people lifted out of poverty. In other words, the estimated poverty-reduction productivity of ODA nearly tripled during the 1990s.

World Bank assistance is, on average, well targeted at reducing poverty.

- IDA is well allocated to places where it will reduce poverty. Even in 1990, much more IDA went to the good-policy countries ($4.7 per capita) than to the poor-policy countries ($2 per capita). By the late 1990s, targeting had improved further, so that good-policy countries now received three times as much aid as poor-policy countries.

- As a result, an additional $1 billion allocated like average IDA in 1997–98 would lift an estimated 434,000 people out of poverty. This means that IDA is not only 60 percent more efficient than it was in 1990, but also 50 percent more efficient than overall ODA.

Well-targeted aid (such as IDA) crowds in private investment by improving the investment climate. As a result, it promotes broader economic growth and has high average overall returns.

- The effects of aid in the right environments extend well beyond poverty reduction.

- Every dollar of IDA flows on average leads to an increase in gross investment of nearly two dollars. In good policy environments, aid also increases foreign direct investment substantially—by 60 cents for each dollar of aid.

- This "crowding-in" effect means that the overall returns to IDA far exceed the direct poverty-reduction returns, and may be as high as 40 percent, according to one study.

Adjustment (or policy-based) lending in the right environments—countries with reasonable policies and strong reform momentum—is effective in accelerating poverty reduction.

- Adjustment lending emerged in the early 1980s as a necessary corrective, in a period when distorted macro environments had undermined the effectiveness of project-level assistance.

- Adjustment lending suffered from early problems with weak commitment and implementation by countries, however, as well insufficient attention to social costs of adjustment. Because each country situation is unique, borrowers need to have sufficient commitment and flexibility to be able to design and sequence reforms appropriate for their circumstances.

- Since its early years, adjustment lending has improved in targeting and design. It is now an effective way of providing strong reform support in countries with adequate policy and institutional frameworks. By the 1990s, it was earning higher evaluation ratings than investment lending.

One lesson from experience is that reform does not usually succeed without strong local ownership and a broad-based approach, which includes a consideration of institutions, governance, and stakeholder participation—a lesson that has provided the impetus for the Poverty Reduction Strategy Paper (PRSP) process.

- At the societywide level, early evidence suggests that the PRSP process is increasing ownership and poverty focus of development programs in low-income countries.

- Although it is too early to gauge outcomes on the ground, full PRSPs are so far associated with a 20 percent increase in pro-poor spending.

4. Effectiveness of Bank Action at the Sectoral, Program, and Project Level

The evolving understanding of development, which we have summarized in chapter 1, is reflected in the changing nature of World Bank activities. Growth has been high on the Bank's agenda throughout the period, and poverty reduction has been an explicit goal since the 1970s. Nevertheless, focal points for the Bank's activities have evolved over the past four decades. In the 1960s, Bank activities included promoting food security; in the 1970s, addressing the energy crisis by encouraging new supplies and conservation; in the 1980s, tackling the debt crisis and promoting open trade policies; and in the 1990s, focusing more on poverty reduction and social development. Over this period the Bank has realigned its work at the sectoral and project level to focus on the quality of the policy environment and to focus on the country as the unit of account. Results have improved over the past decade as the Bank has incorporated its lessons of experience and altered its ways of doing business.

4.1 The Bank has in general achieved high rates of effectiveness at the sectoral, program, and project levels, and these have improved in the past decade, as shown by measured results.

The Bank has substantially improved outcomes on the ground in the past decade. Measurement of these outcomes is reflected in various indicators, such as economic and financial rates of return of Bank-financed projects, growth rates of GDP or sectoral output in countries and sectors supported by adjustment programs, and improvements in social indicators. More systematic tracking of the Bank's results on the ground is being focused on the Millennium Development Goals (MDGs). Country Assistance Strategies (CASs) increasingly set out objectives and measure results on the basis of MDG indicators.

Bank operations on average enhance economic productivity.

Since 1972 the Bank has systematically collected data on project outcomes for every project it has financed and compared these outcomes with the expected outcomes at appraisal. The result is a wealth of data showing outcomes and trends over time by type of project, sector, and country. The older and most frequently used indicators have been the *economic and financial rates of return* of the projects.

The economic rate of return (ERR) is calculated for many projects, though not all: adjustment loans and projects in a number of sectors, such as education, health, and social protection, are not covered. Where they are available, the minimum ex ante economic rate of return (ERR) required of Bank-financed projects is 10 percent. Actual ex post results are considerably better. Figure 4.1 shows the average ERR in the 1990s, by sector, for disbursements in sectors for which sufficient data are available to provide a reliable analysis. The projects represented in the figure cover 47 percent of disbursements for all projects closed during 1996–2001, and 82 percent of disbursements in the sectors included in the analysis. On average, the return on these disbursements was nearly 25 percent, up from 16 percent in the 1980s.

Figure 4.1. Average World Bank ERRs Weighted by Disbursements for Selected Sectors, 1996–2001 (in percent)

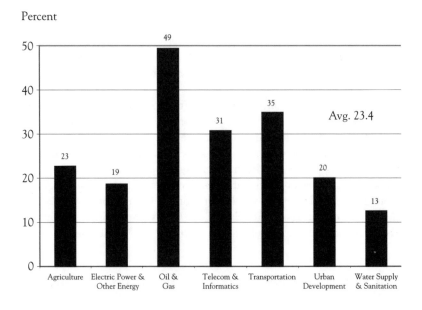

Note: Sectors selected were based on those with at least 15 projects for which ex post ERRs covering at least 20 percent of disbursements were available.

These rates of return demonstrate the positive contribution of Bank-financed projects to increased output and productivity of borrowing countries. Bank research has shown (since about 1990) that individual project outcomes and ERRs are strongly associated with the quality of a country's policy and institutional environment. Evaluation results confirm that the introduction of performance-based lending allocations has contributed to the increase in average ERRs for Bank projects.

The Bank's private-sector arms—the International Finance Corporation (IFC) and the Multilateral Investment Guarantee Agency (MIGA)—also measure their economic impacts systematically. IFC's Operations Evaluation Group (OEG) found that 63 percent of 102 real-sector projects begun in 1993–95 and evaluated near the end of that decade had ERRs in excess of 10 percent. In 65 percent of real sector projects, the ERR exceeded the financial rate of return, meaning that the benefits for customers, employees, suppliers, and taxpayers were greater than the financial benefits to owners and financiers.

Analogously, MIGA's Operations Evaluation Unit (OEU) reported that as of 2000 it had issued 473 guarantees for just over $7 billion, which had facilitated investments of $36 billion; this means that each $1 of guarantee helped to generate more than $5 in investment in developing countries. While some of this investment might have occurred anyway, in a survey of MIGA clients, 73 percent reported that the guarantee was "critical" or "absolutely critical" for their firms to have made the covered investment.[86]

Two caveats are warranted here. Taken alone, these ERRs should be used with considerable caution.

- As noted earlier, if government funds are *fungible*, then the marginal effects of the aid could be far lower than suggested by these calculations. The same is true if private-sector firms would have taken up the project in the absence of Bank action. For these reasons, high ERRs in a sector do not necessarily mean that investment in that sector should be increased.

- On the other hand, if a project is successful at *demonstrating new approaches or making permanent improvements in institutions*, the ERR calculations will be based on underestimates of the project's benefits.

This is why it is essential to complement project-level evaluations with broader evaluations of progress at the sector or country level, as well as cross-country statistical analysis of the type presented in chapter 3. Those earlier results on the effectiveness of IDA lending provide some confidence that these highly positive ERR calculations may at least be of the right magnitude.

Bank lending generally promotes improved health and education in poor countries.

The World Bank has long had projects aimed at improving health and education outcomes in developing countries. The Millennium Development Goals and the CDF/PRSP process (discussed in chapters 2 and 3) have helped raise the profile of these goals still further, so that they are now incorporated more systematically into the preparation of Bank country assistance strategies. A growing number of CASs reflect the objectives and monitor progress against them, and increased lending is going to human development sectors.

Having provided $30 billion for education projects, the Bank is the world's largest external funder of education; it also is the world's largest external funder of health programs, with new commitments of $1.3 billion a year for health, nutrition, and population projects. These social sector projects are achieving large, measurable improvements in human development indicators. (see box 4.1 for examples from the health sector, box 4.2 for an example of AIDS prevention in Brazil, and box 2.1 for an example of progress in both health and education in Bangladesh.)

OED reviews of the health sector portfolio have found that the Bank has made important contributions to strengthening health, nutrition, and population policies and services worldwide.[87] Through its support to policy reform, technical assistance, and financing, the Bank has helped expand geographical access to basic health services, sponsored valuable training for service providers, and contributed advice and other important inputs to government basic health services. The Bank has also used its lending and nonlending services to promote dialogue and policy change on a variety of key issues, including family planning, health financing, and nutrition strategies. Clients appreciate the Bank's broad strategic perspective on the sector, and the Bank has taken a growing role in donor coordination. After an initial focus on

---

Box 4.1. Bank Promotion of Health in Poor Countries: Some Examples

Among the Bank's many initiatives and projects to improve health are the following:

- Lending for HIV/AIDS since 1986 has totaled nearly $1.5 billion, much of that coming after 1998. Box 4.2 shows by way of example what one well-designed Bank-supported program with strong local ownership was able to achieve over a period of several years.

- Bank support for Mali's Health, Population, and Rural Water Project initiated in 1991 led, by the mid-1990s, to a number of gains: the percentage of children fully vaccinated rose from 0 to 24, and overall tetanus and vaccination coverage increased from 18 percent to 50 percent.

- Bank support has helped to address iodine deficiency disorders. In China, for example, a $118 million project in the late 1990s helped raise the proportion of households with adequately iodized salt from 40 to 89 percent between 1995 and 1999, reducing the percentage of 8- to 10-year-olds with iodine deficiency from 13 to 3; ultimately, this is expected to result in average gains of 10 to 15 points in children's IQ levels in affected communities.

---

government health services, the Bank is increasingly focusing on other key issues, such as private and NGO service delivery, insurance, and regulation. In recent years, the Bank also has placed greater emphasis on client ownership and beneficiary assessments in project design and supervision.

At the same time, OED raised a number of shortcomings in the Bank approach to health, such as a slowness to incorporate good institutional analysis into reform design and to focus on improving quality of service. In addition, with some notable exceptions, the Bank has not placed sufficient emphasis on addressing determinants of health that lie outside the medical care system, including behavior changes and cross-sectoral interventions. Promoting health reform required strategic and flexible approaches to support the development of the intellectual consensus and broad-based coalitions necessary for change, and the Bank is in the process of adapting its instruments to place more emphasis on learning and knowledge transfer.

> **Box 4.2. Brazil: Proving that the HIV/AIDS Epidemic Can Be Stemmed**
>
> In the early 1990s, Brazil ranked fourth in the world in terms of reported AIDS cases. To help stem the spread of the deadly disease, the Bank in November 1993 approved $160 million for an AIDS prevention project in Brazil. The AIDS and Sexually Transmitted Diseases (STD) Control Project focused on prevention efforts, but also covered treatment and testing.
>
> Between 1993 and 1997, the project helped 175 nongovernmental organizations carry out more than 400 grassroots campaigns educating high-risk groups such as injecting drug users and sex workers about unsafe or harmful behaviors. The NGOs handed out more than 180 million condoms, raised AIDS awareness among more than 500,000 people, and trained 3,800 teachers and 32,500 students in promoting AIDS and drug abuse prevention.
>
> Aided by another $165 million loan in 1998, the project, now in its second phase, is helping Brazil's Ministry of Health reduce the spread of HIV/AIDS while making it possible for Brazilians with AIDS to live longer, healthier lives. The program has contributed to a *38 percent drop* in the number of AIDS-related deaths since 1993. While supporting special AIDS care clinics and home-care teams to provide treatment for people living with HIV/AIDS, the second phase of the project combats the spread of AIDS and STDs by supporting a nationwide network of 177 AIDS testing and counseling centers and 800 diagnostic and treatment clinics for sexually transmitted diseases. In partnership with the National Business AIDS Council, the Bank's support has enabled 3,000 companies to provide AIDS awareness training to 3.5 million workers.

Bank lending encourages good economic performance.

As Bank lending in support of structural and sector adjustment programs increased after 1980, its results were regularly assessed in several reports. The Bank's internal reviews of the experience of the first decade concluded that, on average, countries that received adjustment lending had moderately higher growth of GDP, imports, and exports than countries that did not. Similarly, evaluations of IFC projects in the 1990s found that 60 percent contributed to overall economic growth in the country.[88] For MIGA projects, nearly half had a substantial or better macroeconomic impact—effects directly related to the size of the project relative to the size of the country's economy.[89]

At the same time, the Bank reviews also found that: (1) failure to address the social costs of adjustment accounted for some policy reversals; (2) supply response in low-income countries (especially in Sub-Saharan Africa) was slow, and more time was required for institutional reforms; (3) there was a need for more specific and monitorable conditionality, particularly for tranche release; and (4) a more selective approach to adjustment lending and closer alignment between the Bank's and countries' expectations were needed.

As highlighted in reports by the Bank and NGOs, although poor people might gain on average from adjustment over the medium term, at least some poor people suffer during the adjustment period; this requires increasing attention to the allocation of public expenditures and cushioning income declines for vulnerable groups.[90] A broader time perspective on the outcomes of adjustment lending, and of the major improvements in the 1990s over the previous decade, is contained in the Bank's recent "Adjustment Lending Retrospective: Final Report" (World Bank 2001b) and "Adjustment from Within: Lessons from the Structural Adjustment Participatory Review Initiative" (World Bank 2001a), as well as in three OED reports.[91] These reports document the mixed experiences of the earlier generation of adjustment operations and the improvements experienced in the 1990s (noted earlier). And they document the increased impact of successful adjustment operations on growth and, particularly, poverty reduction. For example, the share of explicitly poverty-focused adjustment operations increased from 47 percent in 1995 to 75 percent in 1999. In parallel, there has been a growing focus on social objectives: the share of conditions in adjustment loans directly supporting social sector reforms increased from 3 percent in the 1980s to 18 percent in the last three years. Finally, cross-country evidence shows that developing countries receiving adjustment lending in FY90–97 maintained and in some cases increased social expenditures, on average, more frequently than countries without such lending. An example of successful adjustment lending with positive impact on both growth and poverty alleviation is shown in box 4.3.

Outcomes of Bank operations have been improving.

The outcomes of Bank lending are approaching their highest levels in two decades. OED's outcome indicators are performance-related, measuring project contributions to productivity or amelioration of social dimensions of poverty, as discussed above. (The annex of this report

Box 4.3. Uganda: A Successful Poverty-Focused Adjustment Program

One of the better examples of reform has been Uganda, whose story has noteworthy parallels with Vietnam (see box 3.6). The country was estranged from Western donors prior to reforms, and it went through a period when it received little help. The new government in the mid-1980s faced a dire economic situation. Starting with advice, the Bank helped the government learn about policy reform in Ghana and other countries and, in collaboration with multilateral and bilateral agencies, helped it design and implement key measures on fiscal adjustment, exchange rate reform, and trade liberalization. Aid and the conditionality associated with the Bank-supported adjustment lending helped generate and implement policy reforms in the late 1980s and early 1990s, a period during which multilateral assistance from the Bank and other lenders was particularly important. The Bank began disbursing the first of five adjustment operations in 1991.

Since that period, Uganda has achieved a remarkable recovery from the collapse that occurred during the years of civil war, and has increased private investment, reversed capital flight, increased external trade, privatized commercial public enterprises, and—most important—reversed poverty sharply. The results have been very impressive, with poverty (defined as minimum calorie intake) declining from 56 percent in 1992–93 to 35 percent by the year 2000 (Appleton 2001).

While many factors were responsible for this impressive decline in poverty over such a short time period, it appears that the Bank adjustment operations played an important role in at least four areas:

- *The reform program supported by the adjustment operations helped lay the foundation for broad-based economic growth.* Before 1990, annual GDP growth averaged 3.1 percent; after 1990, it averaged 7.2 percent. Much of this increase was due to the impact of successive adjustment programs, which helped slow down inflation, open up trade, achieve exchange rate stability, and reform the overstaffed public sector.

continued

provides more detail about the evaluation system.) Figure 4.2 shows outcome data for nearly 30 years, a period in which standards for good performance have increased, making it more difficult for a project to earn a satisfactory rating. The figure shows a decline in performance from 1977 to 1988, followed by an improvement since then.

Box 4.3. Uganda: A Successful Poverty-Focused Adjustment Program (continued)

- *The reform program helped revitalize coffee and cotton production, on which most poor people depend.* Liberalizing coffee exports and raising cotton prices helped put more income in the hands of poor rural producers. The improvement in the incomes of cash-crop farmers, however, was not accompanied by similar improvements among food-crop farmers. The incidence of poverty among the latter has not changed substantially and requires further attention.

- *The reform program improved the efficacy of school expenditures.* One adjustment loan created a system to monitor the accountability of public funds going to primary schools and school districts.

- *The reform program helped reestablish an improved investment environment.* A major factor in improving the environment for private investment was the effort to return properties to the members of the Ugandan Asian community who had been expelled from the country. This was an exceptional step that stimulated substantial investment from the returning Asian entrepreneurs.

It is important to note that the Ugandan recovery has been just that—a recovery. The economy came crashing down in the 1970s and 1980s, and Uganda spent the 1990s working to return to previously attained levels of development. The challenge now is for the country to develop well beyond the levels it reached in 1970. Doing so will require addressing serious issues of governance, as well as getting social services to function well.

4.2 The Bank has adapted its strategies and projects to improve its performance.

The Bank has achieved improvements in performance over time by continually evaluating, learning, and adapting. Projects are evaluated by the independent Operations Evaluation Department, which reports directly to the Bank's governing board (rather than through the President). In addition, there are systematic analyses of development approaches and project quality carried out by the Operations Policy and Country Services unit (OPCS), the Quality Assurance Group, the Bank's research department, and the thematic networks, all of which help to identify and learn from successes and failures. Through such learning, the Bank has made several major changes in approach that have contributed to improved outcomes over time.

Figure 4.2. World Bank Projects Rated as Achieving Satisfactory Outcomes, 1974–2001

Percent

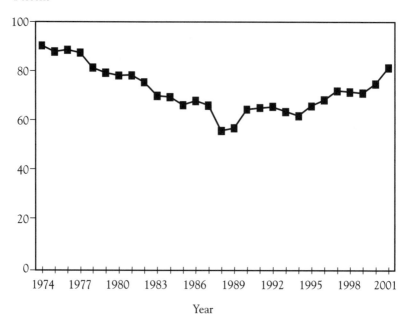

Year

As we explain below, changes in the Bank's approach include: (1) shifts in lending towards human development, social protection, and governance; (2) the introduction of adjustment lending in the 1980s to eliminate major policy distortions; (3) moving beyond projects to adopt the country as the main "unit of account," with Bank's CASs and countries' PRSPs becoming the central framework for ensuring alignment with countries and with the Bank and other external partners; (4) systematic managerial attention to operational quality; (5) tighter social and environmental standards; and (6) improved fiduciary performance. As shown below, these operational emphases have been driven by lessons of experience, new development challenges, and the growing realization that policies and institutions are keys to the effectiveness of development assistance.

**Figure 4.3. World Bank Lending by Network: 1961–2001
(as a percentage of total lending)**

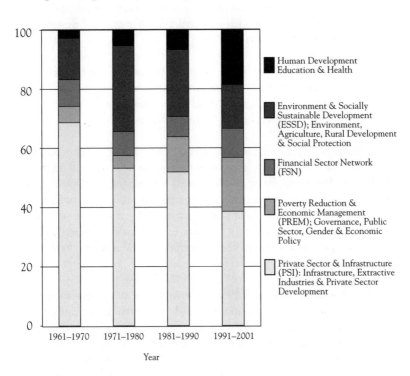

Sectoral and thematic shifts

The Bank has responded to changes in its environment by reallocating its lending. Successful development, plus the growth of international capital markets, meant that emerging markets now had greater access to private finance for revenue-earning development projects, such as transportation and energy. Rather than compete with the private sector, the Bank shifted its efforts—in countries with access to alternative sources of financing—away from financing physical investments to helping countries reform sector policies and establish good regulatory frameworks. There has thus been a sharp decline in the Bank's financing of infrastructure, from about three-fourths of Bank lending in the 1960s to about one-third in the 1990s (figure 4.3). Within the reduced lending for infrastructure, there has been a trend toward more projects—with smaller loan amounts—aimed at helping governments to establish regulatory frameworks, address environmental issues, pilot new approaches to public sector infrastructure delivery, and design mechanisms for private participation.[92]

While the share of lending to the financial sector remained largely constant, the content of the Bank's lending moved from financial intermediary lending through national development banks to supporting financial sector reform and bank restructuring.

In contrast, Bank lending for health, education, and social protection has risen steadily and now constitutes nearly one-fifth of total lending. During the 1990s, the Bank also increased lending for governance and public sector reform, private sector development, and environmental protection. As a result of these shifts, many of which are from the project to program level, Bank projects have become more relevant; but they have also become increasingly complex and demanding for both the Bank and borrower.

The IFC has complemented these shifts in recent years by aiming to crowd in private investment in sectors where private participation holds the most promise. It does this by targeting financial markets, infrastructure, and projects in the social sectors, and "frontier" regions or sectors within countries, as well as high-risk or low-income countries in recent years. In 2001, just under 70 percent of IFC approvals were in targeted sectors and over 40 percent in high-risk or low income-countries.[93]

Evolution of adjustment lending.

Section 3.2 has discussed in detail the evolution of adjustment (or policy-based) lending as a broad instrument of aid, but it is worth reiterating these messages briefly as an example of how the Bank has adapted its approach to improve performance. This type of lending was widely used by the Bank during the early years after World War II, but thereafter the focus shifted to investment lending. Program lending was resurrected in 1980, with the purpose of helping countries adjust their balance of payments after the 1979 oil shock. The focus soon shifted to helping countries remove obstacles to growth as they attempted to overcome the debt crisis of the 1980s. That focus was complemented in the 1990s with an explicit emphasis on poverty reduction and on avoiding adverse social impacts of adjustment. In recent years, as many countries have succeeded in removing major macroeconomic distortions and reducing excessive state intervention, adjustment lending has supported more complex institutional reforms.

The rapid expansion of adjustment lending during the 1980s, and its mixed outcomes during this period, lent great impetus to the learning process. Several OED and Bank reviews analyzed the economic and social impact of adjustment and fed back the lessons learnt into the design of adjustment operations whose results improved greatly. Adjustment operations achieved satisfactory or better outcomes about 60 percent of the time in the 1980s, and above 80 percent in the 1990s—following design improvements and increased country selectivity based on lessons of experience.[94]

Country focus

Along with this increased focus on the policy environment, Bank strategy moved beyond projects to adopt the country as the privileged "unit of account." Although the country had long been at the core of Bank programming, a qualitative change took place in 1990 with the introduction of the CAS. The CAS is a Bank-owned document that sets forth the Bank's assistance program based on the country's own vision and associated development program, the Bank's diagnosis of the country's policies, institutions, and private sector strength, and the Bank's comparative advantage, given the support provided by development partners. The CAS also sets out benchmarks for monitoring and evaluating the Bank's and the country's performance. From 1994, CASs were prepared in consultation with the government and, more recently, participation has been broadened to include NGOs, civil society, the private sector, development partners, and other stakeholders. In 1998, CASs for most countries began to be publicly disclosed. As countries increasingly formulate their visions and programs in PRSPs or other country-owned documents, CASs are expected to acquire more the character of a business plan for the Bank.

Evaluation (including self-evaluation) and borrower feedback have reinforced the country focus by assessing the impact of Bank assistance at the country level. A 1999 Client Feedback Survey found that borrower authorities gave the Bank high marks on: (1) incorporating country realities in project design, (2) technical competence, and (3) ensuring that project benefits justify the cost to the country. Key areas identified for improvement were: (1) building capacity at the community level, (2) strengthening local training and research organizations, (3) helping to strengthen the private sector, and (4) helping to strengthen and maintain sound macro and trade policies.

Enhancing quality management

Experience has demonstrated that for projects to be most successful they should focus on results, respond to client needs, be cost-effective and innovative, and build on the lessons of experience. Evaluations carried out by OED have demonstrated the importance of client commitment to projects, and of client and beneficiary participation in the design and implementation of the project for achieving satisfactory outcomes. (See box 4.4 for an example of a successful project that incorporated these elements.)

Tighter social and environmental standards

The Bank's "safeguard policies" cover its regulations and standards governing the treatment of Environmental Assessments, Natural Habitats, Involuntary Resettlement, Pest Management, Indigenous Peoples, Forestry, Projects on International Waterways, Cultural Property, Safety of Dams, and Projects in Disputed Areas. Management attention to the implementation of these policies has increased in recent years, both as part of the overall quality agenda and as a response to concerns raised by NGOs. For example, a Quality Assurance and Compliance Unit now monitors Bank compliance with its social and environmental safeguards, producing implementation reports for management in real time. On the IFC side, two-thirds of evaluated projects met high standards for environmental sustainability, including many of those whose profitability for their owners fell short.[95]

Inevitably, more rigorous implementation of these policies and compliance monitoring has been seen by some as raising the cost of doing business with the Bank and increasing risk aversion among staff and borrowers, especially with respect to the oversight of the independent Inspection Panel. There is anecdotal evidence that some managers are discouraging their staff from tackling operations

Box 4.4. Elements of a Successful Project: Peru Rural Roads

Based on OED's evaluation criteria, the Peru Rural Roads Project exhibited all of the criteria for successful assistance. The $264 million project was aimed at providing a well-integrated and reliable rural road system through rehabilitation and maintenance of rural roads and building key links to connect with the primary road system. It was focused on results, responsiveness to client needs, cost-effectiveness, and innovation. It contributed to partnership building and demonstrated high levels of professionalism and teamwork.

- The project restored rural people's access to basic social services, improved the availability and affordability of rural transport services, and created entrepreneurial capacity by setting up community-based microenterprises to act as catalysts for furthering local development initiatives beyond the transport sector. The program generated about 32,300 seasonal jobs and 4,700 permanent jobs through the creation of 410 road maintenance microenterprises

- The implementation arrangements of the project took into consideration the views of the various stakeholders. Experimentation, ownership, and trust helped create a responsive working environment where government, international donors, and beneficiaries contributed based on their comparative advantages.

- The project successfully experimented with beneficiary participation in the selection of subprojects and with the use of microenterprises for routine road maintenance. It established a novel framework of institutional collaboration that made the most of the strengths of each stakeholder, including the government counterpart institution, its decentralized executing units, local NGOs, and the Inter-American Development Bank.

- Cooperation was strengthened by the receptiveness of the executing road institution to learning by doing, incorporated feedback throughout implementation, and seeking a more comprehensive response to rural poverty and community development issues.

The original project received OED's top ratings for outcomes, sustainability, institutional development, and Bank and borrower performance. A follow-on project was given the World Bank President's Award for Excellence.

involving safeguard policies, and that the safeguards have reduced the Bank's involvement in some activities, such as sustainable forestry management and construction of major dams. But on balance the safeguard policies have improved the social and environmental quality of Bank operations and have come to be viewed as good-practice benchmarks within the development community.

Improved fiduciary performance

In recent years, the Bank has tripled the resources allocated to ensuring that its funds are used for the intended purposes. The overall quality of fiduciary performance in Bank-financed projects has improved steadily, as the Bank has introduced formal assessments of the financial management and procurement arrangements of the entities that implement individual projects. With the growing importance of nontraditional projects such as adjustment operations and debt relief, it has become clear that fiduciary assurance and achievement of development objectives depend on satisfactory performance in the management of public finances more generally. The Bank therefore has introduced country assessments of financial management and procurement, to provide it with a solid underpinning for its assistance program in each country. Results of the assessments inform the design of assistance programs, including support for measures to address weaknesses revealed by the reviews. At the same time, the Bank is working with international standard-setting organizations to develop a global set of standards for good-quality public financial management.

4.3 The key to the Bank's development effectiveness lies in its attention to both Bank and borrower performance.

The Quality Assurance Group (QAG) evaluates the quality at entry of Bank operations and the quality of Bank supervision. OED evaluates the outcomes of Bank operations and the Bank's own performance—after projects have been completed and all loan funds have been disbursed. QAG's indicators of quality at entry have improved, from 69 percent satisfactory or higher in 1996 to 82 percent in 2001, while OED's have increased from 62 to 79 percent. Since quality at entry is a leading indicator, the performance of completed projects is likely to continue to improve in the next few years. Similarly, an evaluation of IFC projects also concluded that where IFC had done its job consistently well, 90 percent of projects were successful developmentally (compared to 61 percent overall).[96]

A theme running through this paper has been the necessity of learning from both failure and success. This section provides some additional examples of how the Bank has done so.

The Bank seeks to learn from failure.

Development is a risky business and some failures are inevitable. While performance shortfalls have many causes, it is important for the Bank to learn from them and feed that learning back into subsequent operations. Evaluation evidence confirms that when project perform-ance has been weak, the Bank has modified its approach. For exam-ple, Bank lending for power development in Sub-Saharan Africa has been less successful than in other regions. By the early 1990s, evalua-tion had disclosed that power projects were not meeting their goals, especially with respect to financial sustainability. A new sector policy, introduced in 1993 and in force today, identified guiding principles for Bank support in the energy sector. The results in Africa have been impressive: between 1990 and 1994, power outages dropped from 50 to 18 hours per customer per year, losses fell from 20 to 17 percent, and the number of employees per thousand customers decreased from 10 to 7.

A similar learning from costly lessons of experience has been evident in adjustment lending. In line with evaluation lessons, the Higher Impact Adjustment Lending (HIAL) initiative introduced in the Africa Region in 1995 aimed at enhancing adjustment lending through improved country selection and better design. During FY1996–98, HIAL lending to Sub-Saharan Africa (SSA) exceeded US$2 billion through 21 operations in 17 countries. An evaluation of the impacts of the program found that the HIAL group outperformed non-HIAL SSA and all non-SSA IDA countries in terms of fiscal adjustment, exchange and interest rate policy, and structural reforms. The group also achieved better results in terms of macro variables such as infla-tion, current account, foreign exchange reserves, growth, and debt sustainability. Fiscal adjustment was associated with both inflation reduction and growth in the HIAL group. Also, the HIAL share of poverty-focused operations was higher relative to comparators. By enhancing the flexibility of resource flows in HIAL through varied tranching arrangements, governments gained increased freedom in the timing of reforms and greater ownership of programs. A HIAL operation had about half the number of conditions of the SSA average during 1980–93. This is consistent with HIAL's objectives of improving the effectiveness of adjustment lending by providing greater flexibility in disbursement through fewer but more specific conditions.

The Bank aims to build on success.

Sometimes, building on success means helping to *spread successes* across countries and regions through partnership with other development actors. The Green Revolution, which began in South Asia in the 1970s and spread to Africa and Latin America, has led to impressive gains in production of basic food crops across the developing world, as shown in table 4.1. Between 1970 and 1997 yields of cereals in developing countries rose more than 75 percent, coarse grains 73 percent, root crops 24 percent, and pulses nearly 11 percent.[97] The Bank supported this sweeping change through its lending for irrigation, rural infrastructure, and agriculture, and by mobilizing support with other donors through the Consultative Group for International Agricultural Research (described in Section 5.2 below).

At other times building on success results in scaling up a promising initiative. For example, since March 1974 the World Bank has funded, along with the European Union and the World Food Program, five dairy development projects in India. These projects have supported

Table 4.1. Yields of Major Food Crops, Developing Nations (kg/ha): 1970–97

Period	Cereals[a]	Coarse grain[b]	Root crops[c]	Pulses[d]
1970–74	1,523.8	1,114.4	9,393.5	586.6
1975–79	1,744.4	1,307.8	9,976.2	613.2
1980–84	2,056.4	1,498.0	10,472.5	616.0
1985–89	2,259.8	1,558.9	10,868.5	629.1
1990–94	2,486.5	1,753.0	11,201.5	639.4
1995–97	2,673.8	1,930.6	11,653.7	648.8
Change[e]	+75.47%	+73.25%	+24.06%	+10.60%

a. Wheat, rice, other.
b. Corn, barley, rye, oars, millet, sorghum, other.
c. Potatoes, sweet potatoes, cassava, two, yams.
d. Dry beans, broadbeans, dry peas, chickpeas, cowpeas, pigeon peas, lentils, other.
e. Percentage change from 1970–74 to 1995–97.
Source: FAO Statistics **http://www.fao.org**.

Operation Flood, an all-India program begun in the 1960s to promote farmer-controlled dairy cooperatives. By 1996, 10 million farmer members were supplying an average of 11,000 metric tons of milk per day through 55,000 village cooperative societies. This vast organization grew out of a single, small cooperative society. This external support validated government policy changes growing out of a homegrown initiative. An OED impact evaluation found that Operation Flood and the associated policy changes resulted in a spectacular increase in the growth rate of Indian dairy production, from 0.7 percent annually to over 4.2 percent.

Finally, learning from success sometimes means adapting approaches to new challenges. For example, the recognition that local stakeholder participation often is key to development effectiveness has led the Bank to support social funds, a form of lending that allows local stakeholders to determine investment decisions. This is a flexible instrument that can adapt to needs as they arise and as local community groups become aware of the potential source of funding. An OED evaluation concluded that overall this approach has been "highly effective" in delivering small-scale infrastructure efficiently, although the sustainability of service provision is still a challenge.

Country policies matter a great deal in determining outcomes and are a focus for programmatic lending and of analytical work. As discussed in chapter 3, outcomes improve at the country level with increased selectivity. More ODA resources now go to countries with good policies than at the end of the Cold War. In 1990, ODA was unresponsive to policy quality. A country that, compared with its neighbor, had policies and institutions rated one point higher on the Bank's six-point scale could have expected to receive an aid allocation that on average was only 8 percent higher. By 1997–98, the comparable figure was more than 70 percent, demonstrating that aid allocations were now far more responsive to policy and institutional quality.[98] Yet, although the improved selectivity through the 1990s tripled the poverty-reduction effectiveness of ODA, there has not been a corresponding increase in aid levels. Instead, ODA has fallen significantly.

Despite these advances, a lot more remains to be done to improve Bank performance and development impact. Building on the improvement in performance over the 1990s, the Bank continues its efforts to enhance the development impact of its operations. Two areas where the Bank has shown weaknesses, but where progress is now being made, are managing for results and promoting knowledge sharing.

Managing for results

In the late 1990s the Bank increased its focus on results in operational work. It strengthened the systems for ensuring real-time information on the quality and quantity of its lending and nonlending service deliveries to clients as a basis for enhanced management attention to the delivery of development inputs and outputs. It increased its attention to incorporating the lessons of evaluation into the design of new operations and to results-based monitoring and evaluation during project supervision. It also increased its attention to country outcomes in the design and implementation of its Country Assistance Strategies, recognizing the importance of country policies, institutions, and programs, as well as those of other development partners in the actual results. Work is currently underway to strengthen Bank processes and systems for measuring, monitoring, and managing for results, including through use of the Millennium Development Goals.

Sharing knowledge

The Bank has long been engaged in the dissemination of development knowledge through its research program, the World Bank Institute, and its operational programs. Building on technological advances, it can become an even more effective conduit for sharing knowledge on what works in development. Bank potential in this area is substantial given its wide-ranging research, advisory services, publishing activities, training programs, and technical assistance work. More recently, the Bank has developed innovative knowledge-sharing initiatives, such as the Development Gateway, a Web-based information portal. The Bank now needs to manage these activities for results.

Stronger results-based management and innovative approaches to knowledge sharing can position the Bank to better deal with emerging global issues, as discussed in chapter 5.

4.4 Summary

Measured results show that the Bank's actions have been broadly successful, especially over the past decade.

- Bank operations increase **economic productivity** of borrowers. The minimum economic rate of return (ERR) expected from Bank-financed projects is 10 percent. Actual results are considerably better, reaching an average of 16 percent in the 1980s and rising further to 25 percent in the 1990s.

- Bank operations also make a difference in the areas of **health and education.** The Bank is the world's largest external funder of education projects ($30 billion cumulative) and also the world's largest external funder of health programs, with new commitments of $1.3 billion a year for health, nutrition, and population projects. Its projects have had major returns in improved well-being.

- Bank lending encourages **good economic performance.** Reviews of adjustment lending show that in the 1990s, it led governments to maintain their efforts in social areas and poverty focus during adjustment.

- The **outcomes** of Bank lending have improved steadily. Project outcomes, as measured by the independent Operations Evaluation Department, have improved sharply over the past decade. Despite the growing complexity and more demanding nature of its development agenda, the Bank has increased its rate of satisfactory projects from well below 60 percent in the late 1980s to above 80 percent today.

The Bank has increased its effectiveness by incorporating lessons from past experience.

- In response to increases in private capital flows and other developments, the Bank has shifted the **sectoral** composition of its lending, away from direct infrastructure lending (which fell from three-quarters of Bank lending in the 1960s to one-third in the 1990s) and toward the social sectors (now one-fifth of the total).

- It has increased both the quantity and quality of **adjustment** lending. The success rate of adjustment operations has risen from 60 percent in the 1980s to over 80 percent in the 1990s.

- It has improved **quality management,** by identifying the features of successful projects and applying quality control at the early stages of design and implementation.

- It has sharpened its **country focus.** Bank country assistance strategies are now developed in consultation with governments, civil society, the private sector, and other groups, and 55 percent of Bank country directors now live in client countries (compared with none six years ago).

- It has tightened **social and environmental standards.**

- It has improved its **fiduciary performance,** through country assessments of financial management and procurement and fiduciary safeguards at the project level.

The Bank continues to build on its experience and adapt approaches as necessary.

- Development is a risky business, and some failures are inevitable. **The Bank learns from its failures** and the experience of others—for example, by launching a successful Higher Impact Adjustment Lending initiative in Africa in 1995 to improve design and country selection in line with lessons from evaluation, and by changing its approach to the power sector in Africa.

- **The Bank builds on its own successes and those of others** by scaling up promising initiatives, whether its own or those designed and implemented by others. These include the Consultative Group for International Agricultural Research (CGIAR), which contributed heavily to a global Green Revolution that increased yields of major food crops by 75 percent, as well as the high-return Indian dairy cooperative program (Operation Flood).

- The Bank in the late 1990s strengthened its approach to **managing by results,** and also moved strongly to increase **knowledge sharing.** In these areas as in others, there remains room for further improvement.

5. Effectiveness of Global Interventions

5.1 Many global challenges can be handled only at an international level.

Global development challenges—such as loss of biodiversity, deforestation, climate change, and the spread of infectious diseases—cannot be handled solely by individual countries acting at the national level and therefore require multilateral action. As the number and scope of global challenges have grown, so too have the number of actors involved, creating a need for new partnerships and networks among stakeholders. Private charities have become a force in the areas of environment and health. Pharmaceutical companies have become donors to global health initiatives. Private capital flows to developing countries now dwarf official development assistance. The search for international common ground, together with a variety of formal and informal international agreements, have led to new alliances and revised roles for institutions including the Global Environment Facility, World Trade Organization, and the various UN bodies. No single actor can address all of these challenges, and efforts to address them have been growing rapidly.

According to the UN Secretary General's office, hundreds of new programs to address issues of global scope are being created each year. Demand has increased for the World Bank to be proactive at the global level, with donors encouraging the Bank to coordinate selected global efforts. In FY2001 the Bank was involved in over 200 multicountry partnerships, of which 70 were global programs. In FY2001 the Bank spent about $30 million of its administrative budget on the activities of these global programs, provided an additional $120 million in grants from the Development Grant Facility (DGF), and disbursed another $500 million from Bank-administered trust funds.

Although multinational initiatives are required, they often must be linked to country actions. Many of the Bank's global initiatives (see box 5.1) address problems that have both important domestic impacts and major cross-border spillovers, such as financial contagion, the spread of AIDS, ozone depletion, and toxic pollution. Other global problems call for increasing the efficiency of resources spent at the country level through the use of science and technology available only

**Box 5.1. Global Initiatives Supported by the Bank:
Some Examples**

- **Developing new knowledge:** Consultative Group for International
  Agricultural Research, Tropical Disease Research Program, support for
  Global Development Network, and African Economic Research
  Consortium, the leading research group on development

- **Exploiting new technologies:** Global Distance Learning Network,
  Global Knowledge Partnership, InfoDev, Medicines for Malaria
  Venture, World Links

- **Building new networks for assembling and sharing knowledge:**
  Child Labor, Global Forum for Health Research, Global Water
  Partnership, Program for Statistics, Program for Assessing Student
  Achievements, Provention Consortium

- **Involving the commercial private sector:** Global Alliance for
  Vaccines and Immunization, International AIDS Vaccine Initiative,
  Roll Back Malaria

- **Bringing new approaches to private sector development:**
  Consultative Group to Assist the Poorest, Public-Private Infrastructure
  Advisory Facility, Solar Development Group

- **Responding to financial crisis:** Financial Sector Assessment Program,
  Global Corporative Governance Forum, Reports on the Observance of
  Standards and Codes

- **Promoting trade and financial stability:** Capacity Building for
  Agricultural Trade Policy, Integrated Framework for Trade, Financial
  Sector Assessment Program

- **Responding to conflict and post-conflict situations:** Post-Conflict
  Fund

- **Multisectoral responses:** Cities Alliance, Partnership for Child
  Development, UNAIDS

in the richer countries or globally supported research centers, such as
CGIAR. In most cases, complementary national efforts in developing
countries are key to either achieving objectives of the global programs
(such as biodiversity conservation, which often builds on local programs) or ensuring developing countries' access to their benefits (such
as agricultural productivity, where new crop varieties must be matched
to locally adapted cultivation practices).

The Bank's response to these global challenges has been broad and is rooted in a cooperative approach to contribute to global outcomes. Its analytical and advocacy work is helping to accelerate the international trade round for development and to promote support for programs targeted at specific diseases such as HIV/AIDS and malaria.

5.2 Many global programs have been successful.

There is broad-based support for such well-established grant programs as the Global Environment Facility, the Consultative Group for International Agricultural Research (CGIAR), and the Riverblindness Control Program. Many have achieved success, only to face new challenges.

The CGIAR, created in 1971, now includes 16 international agricultural research centers. The 8,500 CGIAR scientific staff work to produce higher-yield food crops; more productive livestock, fish, and trees; improved farming systems; better policies; and enhanced scientific capacity in developing countries. The knowledge generated by CGIAR—and the public- and private-sector organizations that work with it as partners, researchers, and advisors—has paid poor consumers handsome dividends in terms of increased output and lower food prices. More than 300 varieties of wheat and rice and more than 200 varieties of maize developed through CGIAR-supported research are being grown by farmers in developing countries. Food production has doubled, improving health and nutrition for millions. New, more environment-friendly technologies developed by CGIAR have released between 230 and 340 million hectares of land from cultivation worldwide, helping to conserve land and water resources and biodiversity. CGIAR's efforts have helped to reduce pesticide use in developing countries. For example, control of cassava pests alone has increased the value of annual production in Sub-Saharan Africa by $400 million. Yet the CGIAR must now adjust to new realities. Agriculture research technology has changed, giving prominence to molecular biology and genetic approaches. More robust intellectual property rights have produced an explosion in private investment for agricultural research. These changes pose new challenges to the CGIAR size, organization, and approach.

The Onchocerciasis Control Program (OCP) has met its objectives particularly well (see box 5.2). Similarly, the campaign to eradicate smallpox was an international program, and an extremely successful one. In the mid-1960s, when the campaign was launched, smallpox afflicted some 15 million people a year, and it killed 2 million of them; by 1980, the disease had been eliminated.

Box 5.2. Riverblindness Control: Successfully Reaching a Well-Defined Target

Riverblindness or onchocerciasis, a disease widespread in Africa, causes blindness, disfigurement, and unbearable itching in its victims, and has rendered large tracts of farmland in Africa uninhabitable. The Onchocerciasis Control Program (OCP) was created in 1974 with two primary objectives. The first is to eliminate onchocerciasis as a public health problem and as an obstacle to socioeconomic development throughout an 11-country area: Benin, Burkina Faso, Côte d'Ivoire, Ghana, Guinea, Guinea-Bissau, Mali, Niger, Senegal, Sierra Leone, and Togo. The second objective is to leave participating countries with the capacity to maintain this achievement. OCP is sponsored by four agencies: the United Nations Development Program (UNDP), the Food and Agriculture Organization (FAO), the World Bank, and the World Health Organization (WHO).

OCP has now halted transmission and virtually eliminated prevalence of onchocerciasis throughout the 11-country subregion containing 35 million people. Through donations of Mectizan by its manufacturer, Merck and Co, Inc., and financial support from numerous donors, OCP is funded through its conclusion in 2002. By that time, 600,000 cases of blindness will have been prevented, 5 million years of productive labor will have been added to the 11 countries' economies, and 16 million children born within the OCP area will have been spared any risk of contracting onchocerciasis. In addition, control operations have freed up an estimated 25 million hectares of arable land that is now experiencing spontaneous settlement. The OCP program has been hailed as one of the most successful partnerships in the history of development assistance.

More recently, OCP has been assisting beneficiary countries to safeguard this achievement. At the conclusion of OCP in the year 2002, control and monitoring activities will be maintained through a subregional multi-disease surveillance center at the OCP headquarters. The center will participate in training national epidemiologists, creating national surveillance systems, and collaborating with countries for operational research on surveillance. Currently, OCP staff, which is 97 percent African, provides technical and logistical support to participating countries to ensure that they are capable of continuing residual onchocerciasis control activities within the framework of their own national health systems.

A third example of a successful global program is the African Economic Research Consortium (AERC), which is less well known than the first two. Like the riverblindness control program, the AERC is a regional program focused on addressing one of Africa's greatest needs—strong domestic capacity for policy analysis and formulation (see box 5.3). In this case, the international nature of the consortium has made it stronger by allowing a critical mass of researchers and academic institutions, and by encouraging the sharing of experiences across countries.

Box 5.3. Building Domestic Capacity for Policy Analysis in Sub-Saharan Africa

Recent development experience shows clearly that development strategies must be "owned" by the countries that implement them, not dictated by outside donors. But the ability to participate in design and decisionmaking that is necessary for ownership depends on local capacity for policy analysis. For this reason, capacity-building is an essential element of development assistance.

One capacity-building effort that has paid significant dividends is the African Economic Research Consortium (AERC), which was established in 1988 as a research institute and now covers 22 countries. Its secretariat is located in Nairobi. The AERC works to strengthen local capacity for conducting rigorous, independent inquiry into issues affecting economies in Sub-Saharan Africa.

The AERC focuses on improving economic policy through research, training, and dissemination of research findings. The AERC conducts research in-house and administers a small grants program for researchers in academia and policymaking institutions. The AERC has supported 280 research projects, and the number of participating researchers has grown from 40 to 200 since its inception. In addition, biannual meetings hosted by the consortium are among the largest gatherings of professional economists in Sub-Saharan Africa. In addition to its research program, the AERC began in 1992 to administer a two-year collaborative MA program with students and faculty from 20 universities in 15 Sub-Saharan African countries. The program has produced about 800 MA graduates so far, and 200 more students now participate in this program. Many graduates of the AERC have gone on to research and teaching posts throughout the region, and others to high-level positions in African central banks and finance ministries.

continued

Box 5.3. Building Domestic Capacity for Policy Analysis in Sub-Saharan Africa (continued)

Established by six international and bilateral agencies and private foundations, including the World Bank, AERC is now funded by 15 donors, including foundations, governments, and multilaterals. It has a budget of approximately $7 million a year. One measure of the AERC's success is that it has served as an inspiration and model for newer research networks in other regions, such as the Economic Education and Research Consortium, based in Moscow and Kiev, and the Economic Research Forum for Arab Countries, Iran, and Turkey, based in Cairo. Another measure of success is AERC's contribution to improved policymaking in Africa. The three top economic policymakers in Côte d'Ivoire, for instance, are members of the network; and AERC research contributed significantly to the development of Poverty Reduction Strategy Papers in seven African countries (Uganda, Ethiopia, Tanzania, Ghana, Nigeria, Benin, and Kenya). Many of the African participants at the November 2001 ministerial meeting of the World Trade Organization at Doha, Qatar, were AERC graduates, and observers noted that the technical quality of Africa's contribution to these discussions was substantially higher than in analogous meetings a decade or so earlier.

Another more recent global intervention, the Consultative Group to Assist the Poorest (CGAP), has provided performance-based grant assistance to promote the growth of well-managed and sustainable microfinance institutions. Box 5.4 explores this approach and its successes to date. Early OED reviews of CGAP praised its focus on sustainability while also identifying some challenges in such areas as donor coordination and targeting of clients; since that time, the organization has used these evaluation results to refocus as it matured.

5.3 A major challenge, which the Bank is now addressing in collaboration with other partners, has been to improve focus and prioritization.

The number and range of global programs in which the World Bank is involved have increased rapidly over the past five years and has been accompanied by a concern that the Bank may be doing too much, too soon, and too fast. The issue is not whether the Bank should respond to these global issues, but how and to what extent. Looking ahead in their

Box 5.4. CGAP: Providing Performance-Based Aid to Micro Lenders

Microfinance offers valuable lessons for improving the effectiveness of other areas of development assistance, especially those that address development of the private and financial sectors. The Consultative Group to Assist the Poorest, or CGAP—a Bank global initiative—was established in 1995 to help provide assistance to donors active in microfinance. It provides a vehicle for structured learning and dissemination of best practices on delivering financial and other services to the very poor on a sustainable basis. It also attempts to expand the resources reaching the economically active poor, and improves donor coordination for systematic financing of such programs. CGAP has provided performance-based grant support to 60 institutions in 47 countries, for a total of $27 million.

Using its grant fund, CGAP has developed an investment-style approach to grant making that ties tranched funding to institutional needs and performance. The "dividends" or "outputs" to CGAP are the achievement of financial performance measures that will enable that microfinance institution to reach sustainability, and thus reach significant numbers of poor clients. The performance contract that accompanies CGAP's equity-like funding leaves the use of funds entirely at the discretion of management; reporting, monitoring, and continuation of disbursements are tied to the microfinance institution's fulfillment of performance thresholds at the institutional level. These thresholds are designed to lead the microfinance institution to full financial sustainability—that is, the ability to cover all costs including a commercial cost of funds. The thresholds generally step up over time and include indicators such as profitability, efficiency (cost per currency unit lent), portfolio quality, and growth (numbers of clients reached). Because most of a microfinance institution's funding is usually below market rates, achievement of full financial sustainability implies that it will generate substantial surpluses that will be retained to fund yet more services to poor clients.

continued

Prague Communiqué of September 2000, the Bank's Governors endorsed a focused set of priorities for Bank global programs, and these are reflected in the criteria for possible Bank action in global public goods areas:

- that the actions provide clear added value to the Bank's development objectives at the country level;

> **Box 5.4. CGAP: Providing Performance-Based Aid to Micro Lenders (continued)**
>
> CGAP's investment in Compartamos in Mexico illustrates the effect of such leverage. Compartamos works with very poor women in Mexico's most destitute regions. Its early funding consisted mainly of two large grants of $1 million from a private Mexican banker and $2 million from CGAP. Six years later, its client base has multiplied fivefold. More than half of its portfolio of 65,000 borrowers is funded not by grants, but by retained surpluses that it has generated over the period. Now the NGO has invested in a new licensed finance company that will expand the same business. About half of the investment in this finance company came from commercial sources. Under prudential norms, it can leverage the capital of its investors up to five times by selling bonds to the public. Thus, each dollar that CGAP put into Compartamos in 1995 now translates into as much as 20 dollars of microloan service to poor clients. What made this investment successful was that Compartamos kept loan repayment at very high levels and stayed on track to financial sustainability, without abandoning their social mission. Another successful CGAP client is Fondation Zakoura, the second largest microfinance institution in Morocco, which has over 35,000 active clients and has grown rapidly in recent years.

- that the global action by the Bank catalyze resources and build collaborative partnerships;

- that Bank action play to its comparative advantage; and

- that there be an emerging international consensus that the issue calls for global action.

Using these criteria, the Bank has identified five priority areas for global public goods:

- communicable diseases
- environmental commons
- information and knowledge
- trade and integration and
- international financial architecture.

These guidelines are helping the Bank select global programs and have led to new support for activities to combat AIDS and to prevent regional conflicts. These priorities and criteria now need to be incorporated by the Bank in a global strategy for the institution that can guide its global programs, much as—at the country level—the country assistance strategy guides its country programs. As is the case at the country level, this strategy needs to evolve in close consultation with the relevant stakeholders.

5.4 Summary

Many global challenges can be handled only at an international level.

Global development challenges—such as the spread of infectious diseases, the challenge of building an international trade and financial architecture, loss of biodiversity, deforestation, and climate change—cannot be handled solely by individual countries and therefore require multilateral action. Such action is typically most effective when linked to country efforts.

Many global programs have been successful, and greater focus can bring even more success.

One of the most successful programs is the Onchocersiasis Control Program, a collaborative effort of multilateral agencies, governments, NGOs, and the private sector that has eliminated the scourge of riverblindness from an 11-country region of West Africa.

Another important example is the Consultative Group for International Agricultural Research, a network of research centers that has produced more than 500 varieties of grain now planted in poor countries. CGIAR has helped increase average yields in target grains by 75 percent over three decades.

Nevertheless, the expansion of global actions in recent years has led to a recognition that more focus is necessary. The Bank has moved since 2000 to make its global programs more strategic by establishing a small number of priority areas for action; this focus has helped increase the resources available for contributing to high-priority programs, such as combating AIDS and preventing conflict.

6. Conclusions: Learning Lessons to Move Forward

6.1 Summary of findings

In summing up, it is worth emphasizing again the difficulty in proving cause and effect in assessing development assistance. There are several reasons for this: little advancement takes place unless reforms are fully owned by the government, so an external agent like the World Bank cannot and should not take primary credit for the typical reform; successful development assistance requires partnership with other agencies, including civil society, NGOs, and others, both domestic and external; and finally, the most effective development assistance will be catalytic, with effects that spread far beyond the original project or program.

Nevertheless, development assistance has been associated with major successes:

- In health, average life expectancy in developing countries has increased 20 years since 1960. This progress owes much to general economic development that aid has supported, but also to direct interventions such as the vaccination programs that eliminated smallpox.

- In education, illiteracy in the developing world has been halved since 1970. As the world's largest external funder of education, the World Bank has contributed financially to this progress. More important—because external assistance will always be at most a small share of total education spending—the Bank has supported innovative approaches, such as those that have led to better education outcomes in Brazil, Bangladesh, and El Salvador.

- In broader economic development, developing-country growth has on average exceeded that of the developed countries by a small margin since 1990 (and by a large margin in successful reformers). Development assistance has contributed to the acceleration of growth and poverty reduction since the 1980s—a period when the number of people living in poverty worldwide began to fall, after increasing for much of the previous two centuries. Research and analysis pointed the way to better policies, including in such areas as macroeconomics and trade. Moreover, capacity-building and lending provided important support for reforms.

This paper has presented several types of analysis that bolster these conclusions about the effectiveness of development assistance. Cross-country statistical analysis shows that:

- Aid allocation has improved dramatically in recent years, from a poverty-reduction standpoint. The estimated poverty-reduction effectiveness of ODA tripled in the 1990s, thanks largely to the end of the Cold War.

- Well-targeted aid such as IDA crowds in private investment. In both low- and middle-income countries, every dollar of IDA leads to an average increase in gross investment of nearly two dollars, and increases FDI by about 60 cents.

- Well-targeted aid has high economic returns. Because IDA increases overall income as well as reduces poverty, IDA lending has an estimated overall rate of return of up to 40 percent.

Analyses of the experiences of individual countries show that:

- Development assistance contributed to highly successful reform programs in countries as varied as China, Poland, Mozambique, India, Vietnam, and Uganda. These countries have all experienced sharp increases in economic growth, and their reforms have pulled hundreds of millions of people out of poverty.

- In each case, the country and its government were the prime movers for reform, and the main authors of their development strategy. But advisory and capacity-building support also usually played an important role in improving the environment for productivity and poverty reduction early in the reform era. Once the environment was more conducive to growth, the Bank and other donors supported continued reform with larger-scale lending.

Analyses of individual projects showed that:

- Bank operations increase the productivity of borrowers. Bank projects have yielded high returns, with the average economic rate of return rising from 16 percent in the 1980s to 25 percent in the 1990s.

- Measured outcomes of Bank operations have improved steadily, from below 60 percent satisfactory in the late 1980s to above 80 percent today.

And at the global level, the Bank has contributed to successes in areas such as the Green Revolution. CGIAR, a network of research centers that the Bank helped to found, has produced more than 500 varieties of grain now planted in poor countries and has helped increase average yields in target grains by 75 percent over three decades.

There have been some failures in the development experience, and the Bank and its partners have worked to learn from these. For example:

- Structural adjustment lending in the 1980s, though it filled a real need, was far less successful than hoped, due to an overreliance on lending conditionality and an underweighting of social concerns. But as a result of learning, based on both internal analysis and external consultations, Bank performance in structural adjustment has improved: adjustment lending goes increasingly to effective reform governments, and project success rates have climbed sharply.

- Too much support in the 1970s and 1980s went to governments that were not prepared to make the reforms necessary to reduce poverty. They received support anyway for political reasons, most notably during the Cold War.

- Despite the impressive progress in much of Eastern and Central Europe in the 1990s, the transition process in the former Soviet Union has been a wrenching experience. External actors were at first excessively optimistic about short-term prospects, and they placed too little weight on promoting the institutional prerequisites necessary for a market economy. But here too there has been progress: the transition recessions are finally over, and reforms have begun to take root.

There are major challenges remaining. The AIDS epidemic continues to cut life expectancies in Sub-Saharan Africa, undoing decades of progress. In Africa and elsewhere, external actors are struggling with the question of how best to help catalyze and support reforms in the low-income countries that have the poorest policies, institutions, and governance.

Nevertheless, lessons learned are bringing payoffs in improved country performance and better aid allocation, and the end of the Cold War has allowed better targeting of aid at poverty reduction.

6.2 Implications for meeting the Millennium Development Goals

What does this analysis imply for meeting the Millennium Development Goals? One lesson is that external resources alone will not be sufficient to ensure that global goals are met. The recipient country's level of commitment and the quality of its policies and institutions are the primary determinants of progress. Experience and analysis have taught us that outside aid cannot substitute effectively for these factors.

But a second lesson of this paper is that when a country is committed to reform and poverty reduction, external support has substantial payoffs. External support can take several forms including, but not limited to, aid.

One important area where rich countries can provide support is through *reforms of their own trade policies*. The external environment has a strong influence on the returns to reform in developing countries. Robust global growth is important, but so is reform of rich countries' protectionist policies, which target such areas as agriculture and textiles and are thus particularly damaging to poor countries. Open market access to poor countries, combined with other trade reforms, would pull an estimated 300 million people out of absolute poverty, beyond the 600 million who would escape poverty with normal growth.[94]

The second area for support is through direct *development assistance*. The decline in aid flows over the past decade has come precisely at a time when the returns to aid have increased sharply. Section 6.1 has summarized the evidence on returns: if countries are willing to take the steps necessary to reform, then assistance in the form of capacity-building, financial assistance, and analytical support typically has large returns. With continued reform momentum and steady external support, past experience suggests strongly that we can extend and deepen the progress of the past half-century.

Annex

Measuring the World Bank's Development Effectiveness and Managing for Results[100]

In 1992, a World Bank task force on portfolio management analyzed the causes of the declining effectiveness of Bank operations over the preceding decade (see Figure A.1.).[101] The Bank responded with a program of action, but quality levels for completed projects reported by the independent Operations Evaluation Department (OED) continued to stagnate. In December 1995 Executive Directors pointed to the slow pace with which lessons from experience with development assistance were being reflected in new operations. The World Bank's Senior Management then made it its highest priority to restore and enhance the quality of the Bank's assistance and its effectiveness in

Figure A.1. Outcome: World Bank Projects Rated Satisfactory (1974–2001)

Percent

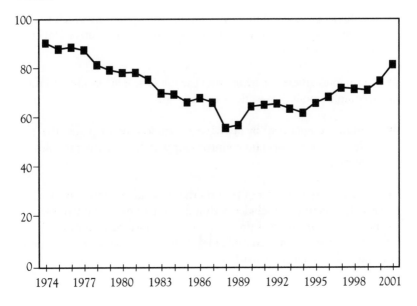

helping countries reduce poverty. This meant a stronger emphasis on managing for results and evaluating the Bank's development effectiveness. This annex presents an overview of the Bank's evaluation methods and criteria, steps taken to address the declining performance measured by evaluation results, and the measured results of those actions.

A.1 The World Bank's evaluation system

The World Bank has developed an increasingly rigorous system of results-based evaluation. This system is designed to provide accountability for the use of Bank resources and to enable the Bank to build on its long experience, so that it might improve its development effectiveness. As part of its efforts to improve the effectiveness of the development system, the Bank works with client countries and collaborates with partner institutions to harmonize evaluation standards and criteria and to build evaluation capacity.

Bank evaluation is keyed to the achievement of results.

The World Bank uses an objectives-based approach to evaluating development effectiveness. This approach has three major advantages:

- it enhances accountability by examining the extent to which the objectives agreed upon with the Bank's Board of Executive Directors have been achieved;

- it promotes efficiency, by relating the use of scarce resources to the accomplishment of specific outcomes; and

- it allows comparisons by applying a common metric across the wide array of sectors and countries for which the Bank provides financing.

This system has a number of features that in combination make it unusually effective: it includes both independent evaluation and self-evaluation; it enables real-time evaluation of ongoing operations; it links to a system of organizational learning; and it uses external expertise and stakeholder participation.

The Bank has well-developed evaluation methods and criteria.

The Bank's major evaluation work uses criteria and a methodology developed by its OED over the last 30 years. Two recent independent reviews sponsored by the Evaluation Cooperation Group, which comprises the heads of the Evaluation Offices of the Regional Development Banks and the World Bank, found that the World Bank's evaluation methods come closest to best practice in the evaluation field. The reviews analyzed the extent to which the major evaluation criteria are appropriately defined and applied.

OED evaluates development interventions by assessing how their results compare with their stated objectives. At the project level, this methodology focuses on the outcomes, sustainability, and impact of Bank operations on institutional development. With different criteria, the methodology has also been extended to country, corporate, sector, thematic, and global policy evaluations.

OED evaluates **outcomes** by considering three factors:

- The **relevance** of the intervention's objectives in relation to country needs and institutional priorities. This factor is particularly important for its ability to identify excessively or inadequately ambitious objectives.

- The **efficacy** of the intervention—that is, the extent to which the developmental objectives have been or are expected to be achieved.

- The **efficiency** of the intervention—that is, the extent to which the objectives have been or are expected to be achieved, using the minimum resources. In addition, the benchmark for a satisfactory investment project is an economic rate of return of at least 10 percent.

Through combining these three factors, overall outcome is rated on a six-point scale, ranging from highly satisfactory to highly unsatisfactory (see box A.1).

OED's **sustainability** measure assesses the resilience to risk of net benefit flows over time by answering four questions:

- At the time of evaluation, what is the resilience to risks of future net benefit flows?

Box A.1. OED's Outcome Rating Scale

Highly satisfactory: All relevant developmental objectives are (or are expected to be) achieved and/or exceeded efficiently, with no shortcomings.

Satisfactory: Most of the relevant development objectives are (or are expected to be) achieved efficiently, with only minor shortcomings.

Moderately satisfactory: Most of the major relevant objectives, on balance, are (or are expected to be) met, although significant shortcomings are observed.

Moderately unsatisfactory: Many of the major relevant objectives are not (or are not expected to be) met; major shortcomings are observed.

Unsatisfactory: Most major relevant objectives are not (or are not expected to be) met and/or most objectives are not relevant.

Highly unsatisfactory: None of the relevant objectives is (or is expected to be) met and/or objectives are not relevant.

- How sensitive is the intervention to changes in the operating environment?

- Will the intervention continue to produce net benefits for as long as intended, or even longer?

- How well will the intervention weather shocks and changing circumstances?

The sustainability of Bank projects has been improving over time, from 48 percent likely in FY1995 through FY1998, to 57 percent likely in FY1999 and FY2000.

The **institutional development impact** measure evaluates the extent to which an intervention improves the ability of a country or region to make more efficient, equitable, and sustainable use of its human, financial, and natural resources. Such improvements can derive from changes in values, customs, laws and regulations, and organizational mandates. Accountability, good governance, the rule of law, and the participation of civil society and the private sector are prominent characteristics of an effective institutional environment. OED evaluates each intervention's success in fostering such changes. Forty-three percent of projects provided substantial institutional development impact in FY2000, compared with about 30 percent in FY1995.

A.2 Bank actions to address declining performance

To address the performance problems observed by the late 1980s, the Bank focused on the building blocks required for ensuring that development assistance contributes to results on the ground: the quality and delivery of operations (doing things right); the quality of country assistance strategies and sector strategies (doing the right things); effective guidance to staff through operational policies; and an allocation of administrative resources that reflects and supports a results orientation. In these efforts, the Bank uses the results of both self-evaluation[102] and independent evaluation by OED as a means of continuous learning and for holding managers accountable. While concentrating on the building blocks, the Bank is also paying attention to measuring the institution's performance in partnering with other organizations to help countries achieve the Millennium Development Goals.

The Bank has improved the quality of operations.

To turn around the quality of operations, management has clarified accountabilities, ensured real-time feedback through a Quality Assurance Group (QAG), set targets for improvement in areas of lagging performance, and provided support to task teams. As a result, there has been a continuous improvement in the active portfolio.[103] Between FY1996 and FY2000, quality at entry increased from less than 70 percent satisfactory to 90 percent (figure A.2). Meanwhile, the quality of supervision rose from 63 percent satisfactory to 92 percent (figure A.3), and the share of projects at risk fell from 29 percent to just 15 percent (figure A.4). The Bank's efforts to enhance effectiveness are continuing with a focus on promoting the wider use of monitoring and evaluation in Bank operations, strengthening the evaluation capacity of developing countries, and standardizing Bank processes for identifying and managing risks.

The Bank has strengthened nonlending services.

The management of the Bank's economic and sector work (ESW) also has been strengthened in response to concerns about declining quality

Figure A.2. QAG Trends in Quality at Entry
(percent satisfactory or higher)

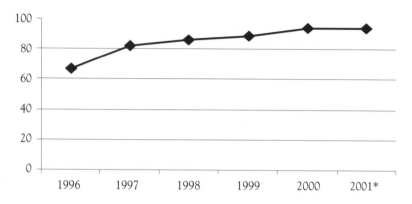

Figure A.3. World Bank Projects with Satisfactory Supervision
Quality (percent)

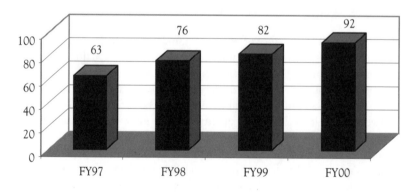

and coverage.[104] Accountability for strategic content, delivery, costs, and quality of ESW products has been strengthened, and the Bank is closely monitoring the implementation of the ongoing ESW program. This attention has already brought about an increase in quality, with the share of products rated satisfactory or better increasing from 72 percent in FY1998 to 86 percent in FY2000.[105]

Figure A.4. World Bank Projects and Commitments at Risk (percent)

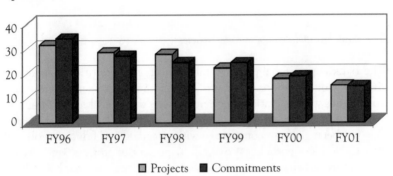

☐ Projects ■ Commitments

The Bank has developed operational strategies.

The Bank establishes its operational strategies through Country Assistance Strategies (CASs) and Sector Strategy Papers (SSPs). Introduced in FY1991, CASs evolved into strategic documents in the mid-1990s as the Bank shifted its focus from projects to supporting countries in achieving their own vision for growth and poverty reduction. Regular CAS retrospectives were introduced to advance the process. CASs now reflect lessons learned and use the Bank's comparative advantage as a criterion for assessing how the Bank might work most effectively with its partners in helping countries achieve their objectives.[106] The latest retrospective documents quality improvements along several dimensions, notably the treatment of governance and participation, the social and political underpinnings of reform, poverty issues, and the incorporation of lessons from independent evaluation and self-evaluation. Bank management pays particular attention to weaknesses reported in the retrospective and OED's independent CAEs—including, notably, risk analysis.

SSPs were introduced in FY1997 to clarify the Bank's role in the sectors, review lessons of experience (drawing on self-evaluation, independent evaluation, and research results produced inside and outside the Bank), identify issues, define strategic directions, and recommend actions. Management has conducted its own stocktaking of the quality of SSPs, and is taking measures to better align new SSPs with emerging corporate priorities, improve the treatment of risk, and improve the coordination of country and sector strategies.

The Bank has updated operational policies.

The Bank's operational policies embody corporate priorities and guide the design of operations. Management's emphasis has been on ensuring compliance with operational policies, which was crucial for moving the Bank from a culture of approval to a culture of results. Particular attention has been given to compliance with safeguard and fiduciary policies. QAG has reported that overall, 87 percent of projects were rated satisfactory or better for supervision of fiduciary and safeguard aspects in FY2000, up from 82 percent in FY1997. To further strengthen compliance, the Bank established a new Quality Assurance and Compliance Unit (QACU) to provide staff with authoritative, consistent, and timely advice on the application of all safeguard policies.

In the past, policies typically included a mixture of requirements and advice to staff, leading to uncertainty about implementation. Bank management therefore introduced a new framework of Operational Policies/Bank Procedures that clearly separates requirements from advice. The revision of policies is a continuous process of adding, discarding, and updating, aided by drawing on the lessons of experience. For example, the Operational Directive on adjustment lending issued in 1992 has been complemented in recent years by three Operational Memoranda with instructions to staff on adjustment operations. Lessons were distilled in a recent retrospective,[107] which serves as the basis for work to revise the existing directive in the Operational Policy/Bank Procedure format. Management guides this process with a view to avoiding disruption in the work of operational staff and ensuring implementation.

The Bank has adopted performance-based resource allocation.

Retrospective analysis shows that country budgets are being more tightly linked with poverty and country performance. This reflects an increasing use of comparative and benchmarking tools at several levels of the planning process. The most widely used model relates budgets to performance, population, and poverty as the main variables. Used at the country level, it helps achieve an allocation of resources that is both fair to the country-specific situation and consistent with the corporate strategy. In addition, at the regional level, there is an increasing reliance on regional compacts. By linking anticipated outputs explicitly with unit budget envelopes, the compacts contribute to results-based management and further unit cost-effectiveness.[108]

Bank management has initiated work on a budget reform starting with a review of, among other things, the criteria and processes for determining country and sector board budgets. One objective of this work is to better link resource allocation to results.

Bank outcomes have been improving.

As figure A.1 shows, the outcomes of Bank lending are approaching their highest levels in two decades, despite more strenuous evaluation standards. From a low of 57 percent in 1988, the percentage of projects rated satisfactory by OED rose to 82 percent in 2001. Most of these gains were achieved after 1996, reflecting the actions discussed above.

A.3 Conclusions

The Bank's evaluation and control system, which helps set the standard within the development community, is results-oriented, objective, rigorous, and comprehensive. It operates under the oversight of the Board, backed by the independent Operations Evaluation Department. It provides real-time, high-quality data that are used to manage development risks. It is linked to policymaking, organizational learning, and knowledge management; and it is in constant evolution to reflect changing corporate priorities and needs.

The evaluation and control system has contributed to the Bank's renewal over the past five years. Overall, the development effectiveness of Bank operations has improved, and development effectiveness has been enhanced through a stronger country focus, improved responsiveness, and enhanced operational quality. Increasing demands at the country and global levels, expanding roles for capacity building and aid coordination, and the increasing complexity of operations nonetheless require that the Bank intensify its efforts to enhance its evaluation skills, instruments, processes, and relationships.

The need to demonstrate results, especially in the area of reducing poverty, requires that the World Bank, in consultation with its development assistance partners and developing country members, continue to place a high priority on enhancing its evaluation capacity. The Bank accordingly has initiated work to enhance the monitoring and evaluation of country-based poverty reduction programs, through capacity building and evaluation harmonization efforts linked to the PRSP initiative.

Notes

1. This paper was prepared under the direction of Nicholas Stern, chief economist and senior vice president, Development Economics (DEC), and Ian Goldin, director of Development Policy. Halsey Rogers, a senior economist, was the lead author. Chapters 4 and 5 draw heavily on the experience of the Operations Evaluation Department; the interpretation of the material is the responsibility of DEC. The research team is grateful for the contributions, comments and assistance of many people. Gregory Ingram and Patrick Grasso provided essential contributions and insights throughout the preparation of the paper. Coralie Gevers and Amy Heyman made many valuable contributions. Lawrence MacDonald provided helpful editorial guidance. Others who provided inputs and comments include: Sadiq Ahmed, Martha Ainsworth, Robert J. Anderson, Caroline Anstey, Oscar Avalle, Rema Balasundaram, Amar Bhattacharya, Sara Calvo, Chiraporn Chotikabukkana, Paul Collier, Louise Cord, Deborah Danker, Angus Deaton, Shanta Devarajan, David Dollar, Eduardo Doryan, Clara Else, Bernd Esdar, Shahrokh Fardoust, Alan Gelb, Egbert Gerken, Daniela Gressani, Stephen Howes, Assaad Jabre, Asma Jahangir, Keith Jay, Olga Jonas, Ioannis Kessides, Homi Kharas, Pierre-Joseph Kingbo, Jeni Klugman, Kathie Krumm, Geoff Lamb, Patricia Laverley, Uma Lele, Zita Lichtenberg, Johannes Linn, Kevin Lu, Frank Lysy, Callisto Madavo, Ernesto May, Pradeep Mitra, Peter Moll, Carlos Mollinedo-Trujillo, Mustapha Nabli, Govind Nair, Dorota Nowak, Anthony Ody, Douglas Pearce, Manuel Penalver, David Peretz, Guillermo Perry, Robert Picciotto, Amedee Prouvost, Oliver Rajakaruna, Maria Ramos, Mamphela Ramphele, Teja Raparla, Martin Ravallion, Ritva S. Reinikka, Joanne Salop, Jean-Louis Sarbib, Amartya Sen, Nemat Shafik, William Shaw, Veena Siddarth, Anil Sood, Joseph Stiglitz, Rebecca Sugui, Helen Sutch, Kotaro Suzumura, Svet Tintchev, Hasan Tuluy, Ko-Yung Tung, and John Underwood, as well as Ken Rogoff and his colleagues in the Research Department of the IMF. The participants at a seminar with InterAction provided very useful suggestions on the outline. Finally, while this paper, as a research paper, was not subject to clearance by the Executive Board of the World Bank, the research team would also like to thank the Executive Directors of the Bank for their excellent comments on the draft.

2. Data are taken from the World Bank's SIMA database and from World Bank (2002b).

3. The quality and coverage of the household survey data used to measure poverty have improved dramatically in the last 10 to 15 years, and the Bank has played an important role in facilitating this improvement. The Bank's "$1/day" poverty estimates since 1990 have drawn fully on these new data. However, the paucity of adequate survey data back in time naturally makes

estimation over longer periods more hazardous. In *Globalization, Growth, and Poverty*, it was estimated that the number of people living below $1/day had fallen by 200 million between 1980 and 1998. As noted in the report, that estimate had to be based on two different sources, which used different methods. Further checks using more consistent methods corroborate the earlier estimate. These estimates also suggest that without China there would have been little or no net drop in the total number of poor.

4. More than half the world's population still lives on less than $2 per day, an alternative poverty line close to the national line used in many countries. Nevertheless, the share living in poverty by this measure has also declined sharply over the past decade, from 62 percent to 55 percent. In the case of the $2/day poverty line (although not the $1/day line), most of the reduction in global poverty share since 1990 is attributable to China's rapid growth (World Bank, 2001f).

5. The effective World Bank support for the education sector is considerably larger than this, because some broader policy-based lending includes support for education-sector reforms. Even calculated this way, however, the resources that the Bank can possibly provide in support of education are dwarfed by the needs of developing countries.

6. Although our knowledge has already expanded significantly in this area, the World Bank has recently taken steps to accelerate its learning by establishing a Task Force on Low-Income Countries under Stress. That task force will soon be delivering its report. More details can be found in Section 3.1 of this paper.

7. In discussions of the raison d'être of the World Bank, John Maynard Keynes envisaged the organization's primary duty as reconstruction of war-torn economies. Between 1946–1948, the Bank had lent $497 million ($2 billion in constant 1995 US$), mostly in the form of reconstruction credits. In May 1947, France became the first loan recipient, and soon after, similar loans were approved for Denmark, Luxembourg, and the Netherlands (Kapur, Lewis, and Webb 1997, Chapter 2).

8. World Bank (2000e), Sen (1999).

9. Based on Stern (2001), Collier, Dollar, and Stern (2001).

10. World Bank (2001h).

11. This section draws on various surveys, including Barro (1991), Barro and Sala-I-Martin (1995), Rodrik (2001), and Easterly and Levine (2001).

12. Fischer (1993).

13. Sachs and Warner (1995), Frankel and Romer (1999).

14. World Bank (2001f). Although this result is simply a correlation and does not prove causation, faster economic growth and productivity increases could be causing greater export competitiveness, rather than the other way around. The Frankel and Romer (1999) paper cited above attempts to get around this problem by looking at exogenous factors (specifically, geography) that lead to higher trade levels and then looking at differences in growth rates.

15. Levine and Renelt (1992).

16. Easterly and Levine (2001).

17. Devarajan, Easterly, and Pack (2001) make this point in the African context.

18. Krueger and Lindahl (1999), Hanushek and Kim (1995).

19. In an environment of weak institutions, widespread corruption, or lawlessness, additional education may simply make the average worker more effective at rent-seeking or illegal activities.

20. World Bank (2001d).

21. Rodrik (2001), World Bank (2001h).

22. World Bank (2001c).

23. Romer (1994).

24. Dutz and Hayri (2000) provide some evidence on the role of competition authorities in spurring productivity growth.

25. Canning, Fay, and Perotti (1994) provide evidence on the effects of infrastructure on growth. Various studies (such as Collier and Gunning 1995) have cited poor infrastructure as a major reason for poor African economic performance.

26. Issue paper jointly prepared by the African Development Bank, the Asian Development Bank, and the World Bank for the Third United Nations Conference on the Least Developed Countries, Infrastructure Development Session, May 2001.

27. Chong and Hentschel (1999).

28. Gallup, Sachs, and Mellinger (1999), World Bank (2002b).

29. Collier and Gunning (1995).

30. Pritchett (2000), Easterly (2001)

31. This section draws heavily on World Bank (1998b, 2000e) and Dollar and Kray (2001).

32. World Bank (2002b).

33. World Bank (2000b), p. 91.

34. Ravallion (2001) analyzes the variation behind this average relationship.

35. World Bank (2000e), p. 54.

36. For example, a devaluation tends to benefit poor farmers producing cash crops, but the resulting price increase may hurt the urban poor, at least in the short term.

37. World Bank (2000e), Narayan and Petesch (2002).

38. World Bank (1998b), p. 17.

39. Krueger and Lindahl (1999) summarize the evidence.

40. Note that for expositional clarity, all countries' incomes in 1970 are indexed to a value of 100. The "high group" includes China, Botswana, the Republic of Korea, Singapore, Hong Kong (China), Thailand, Mauritius, Malaysia, Indonesia, and Egypt. The "low group" includes Chad, Haiti, Central African Republic, Venezuela, Madagascar, Zambia, Niger, Kiribati, Nicaragua, and Sierra Leone.

41. Claeson and others (2001).

42. In China, for example, per-capita incomes increased by less than a third in the 130 years between 1820 and 1950 (World Bank 1997, citing Maddison 1995).

43. See, for example, World Bank (1993).

44. World Bank (2002b).

45. Collier, Dollar, and Stern (2001), World Bank (2002b), calculations from World Bank data.

46. IBRD lending was resumed in 1997 and 1998 to help Korea deal with the East Asian financial crisis. In view of the subsequent rapid economic recovery and Korea's regained access to capital markets, the Korean government and the Bank have agreed on a new phase of cooperation based on nonlending services, underpinned by a Memorandum of Understanding for a Knowledge Partnership.

47. Of course, there is a continuum of performance, and the precise dividing line between these groups of countries is to some extent arbitrary. Nevertheless, it is clear that development progress has varied widely across countries, and policies and institutions are linked with performance.

48. AIDS also threatens gains in education, in part due to the loss of teachers to the epidemic.

49. World Bank (2000b).

50. World Bank (2002c).

51. See, for example, Boone (1996); note, however, that Hansen and Tarp (2000 and 2001) find the contrary.

52. Owens and Hoddinott (1998).

53. This section is based heavily on World Bank (1998a) and Collier and Dollar (2001a).

54. Some recent analyses have confirmed the importance of aid but failed to find the strong link between aid effectiveness and policy environment shown in the research cited earlier; see, for example, Hansen and Tarp (2000 and 2001). For this reason, the numbers on aid effectiveness cited here should be taken as approximations. Nevertheless, the cross-country evidence on an aid-policy interaction is borne out strongly by case study research such as Devarajan, Dollar, and Holmgren (2001).

55. World Bank (1998a) makes this point, providing a useful set of hypothetical examples and summarizing the empirical evidence (Chapter 3). It notes that because of fungibility, Feizioglu, Swaroop, and Zhu's (1998) cross-sectional study of 14 countries found that the net effect of a dollar's worth of aid to agriculture was a slight decrease in spending on agriculture.

56. Figures in this section are drawn primarily from Collier, Devarajan, and Dollar (2001).

57. Dollar (2000).

58. Devarajan, Dollar, and Holmgren (2001).

59. These calculations are based on cross-country regressions that correlate aid with improvements in growth and poverty reduction, after adjusting for policy and other variables; see Collier and Dollar (2001a, 2001b) and Collier, Devarajan, and Dollar (2001) for details.

60. In 1997, the most recent data available, government expenditures for high-income OECD countries accounted for 29.5 percent of total GDP. Assuming that this relative level of spending continued through 2000, when their total GDP was $24.073 trillion, total government spending was $7.1 trillion. Total ODA in 2000 was $53.7 billion. So ODA as a share of government expenditures was 0.76 percent.

61. Collier, Devarajan, and Dollar (2001); see also note 59.

62. The table shows overdues of over 180 days (that is, in "nonaccrual status"). As of October 2001, IDA borrower countries in nonaccrual status were Afghanistan, Côte d'Ivoire, Democratic Republic of Congo, Haiti, Myanmar, Liberia, Somalia, Sudan, and Zimbabwe.

63. The senior status of World Bank debt clearly deserves much of the credit for high repayment rates: countries will generally not default or even be late on their Bank loans if they have other options. Nevertheless, these statistics are useful as an indication that, contrary to some perceptions, countries are generally in sufficiently good economic shape after borrowing that they are able to meet their repayment schedule.

64. World Bank (1998a), Collier, Devarajan, and Dollar (2001).

65. Collier, Devarajan, and Dollar (2001). Collier and Dollar (2002) estimate that, for a country with average policy and aid levels, ODA has a rate of return of 20 to 30 percent.

66. World Bank (1994a).

67. This section is based on the upcoming World Bank report (still in draft) on the findings of the Task Force on Low-Income Countries under Stress (LICUS). It should be noted that the more successful countries did benefit from extensive support from the international community, including the World Bank; boxes in this report describe the Bank's role in providing knowledge and then lending support (both adjustment and investment) to Uganda and Mozambique. Nevertheless, within the LICUS group, these countries were exceptional in their commitment to reform.

68. Devarajan, Dollar, and Holmgren (2001).

69. World Bank (2000a).

70. More specifically, adjustment lending began in 1980 with the purpose of helping developing countries adjust their balance of payments after the 1979 oil-price shock. With the advent of the debt crisis in 1982, the focus of adjustment lending shifted from fiscal adjustment in response to external shocks to removing obstacles to growth, with the idea of enabling countries to grow out of debt. The focus on growth was complemented in the 1990s with an explicit emphasis on poverty reduction to ensure that the benefits of growth reached the poor and that adverse social impacts of adjustment were avoided. As many countries have already removed basic macroeconomic distortions and have liberalized markets, in recent years adjustment lending has increasingly supported more complex institutional reforms, particularly in middle-income countries. As a result, the share of policy conditions supporting trade, exchange rate, and monetary policy reforms has declined from 31 percent in FY1980–88 to 12 percent in FY1998–2000, and the share of conditions applied to infrastructure, energy, and agriculture has declined from 22 percent to 5 percent. In contrast, over the same period the shares of conditions supporting reforms in other areas increased—from 15 percent to 24 percent in public sector management, from 28 percent to 41 percent in the financial and private sectors, and from 3 percent to 18 percent in the social sectors. Across all sectors, the reform issues supported by adjustment lending are increasingly long-term and of an institutional nature. See World Bank (2001b).

71. See, among others, Stewart (1995), Sahn (1996), and Killick (1999).

72. Dollar and Kraay (2001), Ravallion and Chen (1997).

73. World Bank (2001b).

74. A study by OED on the adjustment lending experience of 23 countries between 1980 and 1983 reveals that adjustment programs were not successfully implemented in about a third of these countries. A similar result emerges from a study of 220 adjustment loans mostly approved in the same period. See Jayarajah, Branson, and Sen (1996) and Dollar and Svensson (1998).

75. Examples of countries that successfully implemented reform programs with the support of adjustment lending during the 1980s and early 1990s include Ghana, Mauritius, Thailand, Korea, Argentina, and Peru. In Ghana, annual per capita income growth turned from -1.6 percent in 1961–83 to 1.4 percent in 1984–94. Annual per capita growth rates between 1980 and 1984 amounted to 4.3 percent in Mauritius, 5.3 percent in Thailand, and 6.7 percent in Korea.

Argentina and Peru made failed reform attempts during the 1980s, but achieved successful reforms after 1990. Per capita growth responded: in Argentina it turned from -1.9 percent annually in the 1980s to 4.7 per year in 1990–94, and in Peru from -2.6 percent to 2.6 percent in the same periods. See Easterly (2001).

76. See, for instance, Johnson and Wasty (1993).

77. World Bank (1998a), International Monetary Fund (1998).

78. Devarajan, Dollar, and Holmgren (2001).

79. World Bank (1998a).

80. It should be noted that different studies have come to different conclusions on this point (see World Bank 2001a for a summary), but also that the evidence that adjustment harms some poor people is fully consistent with the conclusion that on average the poor benefit from reform.

81. World Bank (2001b).

82. It is important to note that the current success rates are nearing the upper limit of what is desirable. A success rate of 100 percent would likely indicate that the Bank was taking too few risks; as noted in the text, development is inherently a risky business, and some potentially high-return forms of external assistance will also be high risk.

83. World Bank (1996b).

84. International Monetary Fund and World Bank (2002).

85. Poverty-reducing spending is country specific and follows the definition in the PRSP or the I-PRSP (interim PRSP). Data are drawn from the PRSPs themselves or from other documents (such as staff reports or decision point documents). Among poverty-reducing expenditure items that are common to the countries in the sample are primary health care spending, primary education spending, water and sanitation, roads, and rural development.

86. West and Tarazona (2001).

87. World Bank (1999b, 1999d, 2000a).

88. International Finance Corporation (2001).

89. West and Tarazona (2001).

90. See, for example, Watkins (1995).

91. World Bank (1994b, 1996a, 1999c).

92. In India, where there are decades-old fiscal problems rooted in the power sector, the Bank helps reform-minded states dismantle bankrupt State Electricity Boards, privatize generation and distribution, and put in place new pricing and regulatory policies.

93. International Finance Corporation (2002), pp. 25 and 29.

94. These improvements have most recently been documented in the Adjustment Lending Retrospective (World Bank 2001b). It should be noted that some observers, including NGOs, continue to raise questions about the social impacts of structural adjustment programs, arguing that the use of this average satisfactory rate does not properly capture the difficult experiences of some countries.

95. International Finance Corporation (2002), p. 14.

96. International Finance Corporation (2002), p. 9.

97. World Bank (1999e).

98. Dollar (2000).

99. World Bank (2001f).

100. This annex was prepared by staff in the Operations Evaluation Department (OED) and the Operational Policy and Country Services vice presidency of the World Bank.

101. See World Bank (1993).

102. The World Bank uses a variety of self-evaluation tools, including self-evaluation in the context of project status reports, project completion reports, and CASs, as well as reviews by the Quality Assurance Group (QAG), and periodic retrospectives of CASs, economic and sector work (ESW), and lending produced by the Operations Policy and Country Services unit (OPCS). More broadly, the Bank's research and its ESW analyze experience with the Bank's approaches to development assistance.

103. See World Bank (various years).

104. See World Bank (2000c, 2001e).

105. See World Bank (2001g).

106. See World Bank (1999a).

107. See World Bank (2001b).

108. The increase in budget for the Africa region in FY2002 can illustrate how these tools complement each other. Based on an analysis of the relative poverty and performance of individual countries in this region, an additional budget was proposed. To manage this shift, this extended envelope was then embodied in the region's compact that included an explicit increase in deliverables.

References

Appleton, Simon. 2001. "Changes in Poverty and Inequality." In Ritva Reinikka and Paul Collier, eds. *Uganda's Recovery: The Role of Farms, Firms, and Government.* Washington, D.C.: World Bank.

Barro, Robert. 1991. "Economic Growth in a Cross Section of Countries." *Quarterly Journal of Economics* 106: 407–443.

Barro, Robert, and Xavier Sala-I-Martin. 1995. *Economic Growth.* New York: McGraw-Hill.

Boone, Peter. 1996. "Politics and the Effectiveness of Foreign Aid." *European Economic Review* 40(2): 289–329.

Canning, David, Marianne Fay, and Roberto Perotti. 1994. "Infrastructure and Growth." In Mario Baldassarri, Luigi Paganetto, and Edmund Phelps, eds. *International Differences in Growth Rates: Market Globalization and Economic Areas.* New York: St. Martin's Press, pp. 113–47.

Chong, A., and J. Hentschel. 1999. "Bundling of Basic Services, Welfare and Structural Reform in Peru." Processed. The World Bank Group, Washington, D.C.

Claeson, M., C.C. Griffin, T.A. Johnston, M. McLachlan, A.L. Soucat, A. Wagstaff, and A.S. Yazbeck. 2001. "Poverty Reduction and the Health Sector." In *Poverty Reduction Strategy Sourcebook.* Washington, D.C.: World Bank.

Collier, Paul, Shantayanan Devarajan, and David Dollar. 2001. "Measuring IDA's Effectiveness." Processed. World Bank, Washington, D.C.

Collier, Paul, and David Dollar. 2001a. "Development Effectiveness: What Have We Learnt?" Processed. Development Research Group. World Bank, Washington, D.C.

———. 2001b. "Aid, Risk and the Special Concerns of Small States." In *Global States and the World Economy.* Commonwealth Secretariat.

———. 2002. "Aid Allocation and Poverty Reduction." *European Economic Review* (forthcoming).

Collier, Paul, David Dollar, and Nicholas Stern. 2001. "Fifty Years of Development." In Nicholas Stern, ed., *A Strategy for Development.* Washington, D.C.: World Bank.

Collier, Paul, and Jan Gunning. 1995. "War, Peace and Private Portfolios." *World Development* 23(2): 233–41.

Devarajan, Shantayanan, David Dollar, and Torgny Holmgren, eds. 2001. *Aid and Reform in Africa.* Washington, D.C.: World Bank.

Devarajan, Shantayanan, William R. Easterly, and Howard Pack. 2001. "Is Investment in Africa Too Low or Too High?" *Journal of African Economies* 10: 81–108.

Dollar, David. 2000. "Has Aid Efficiency Improved in the 1990s?" Processed. World Bank, Washington, D.C.

Dollar, David, and Aart Kraay. 2001. "Growth is Good for the Poor." Policy Research Working Paper 2587. World Bank, Washington, D.C.

Dollar, David, and Jacob Svensson. 1998. "What Explains the Success or Failure of Structural Adjustment Programs?" Development Research Group. World Bank, Washington, D.C.

Dutz, Mark, and Ayden Hayri. 2000. "Does More Intense Competition Lead to Higher Growth?" Policy Research Working Paper 2320. World Bank, Washington, D.C.

Easterly, William. 2001. *The Elusive Quest for Growth: Economists' Adventures and Misadventures in the Tropics.* Cambridge, Mass.: MIT Press.

Easterly, William, and Ross Levine. 2001. "It's Not Factor Accumulation: Stylized Facts and Growth Models." Unpublished paper. World Bank, Washington, D.C.

Feizioglu, Tarhan, Vinaya Swaroop, and Min Zhu. 1998. "A Panel Data Analysis of the Fungibility of Foreign Aid." *World Bank Economic Review* 12(1): 29–58.

Fischer, Stanley. 1993. "The Role of Macroeconomic Factors in Growth." *Journal of Monetary Economics* 32(3): 485–512.

Frankel, Jeffrey, and David Romer. 1999. "Does Trade Cause Growth?" *American Economic Review* 89(3): 379–99.

Gallup, John Luke, Jeffrey Sachs, and Andrew Mellinger. 1999. "Geography and Economic Development." *Annual Bank Conference* on *Economic Development 1998*, pp. 127–78. World Bank, Washington, D.C.

Hansen, Henrik, and Finn Tarp. 2000. "Aid Effectiveness Disputed." In Finn Tarp, ed. *Foreign Aid and Development: Lessons Learnt and Directions for the Future.* London: Routledge.

———. 2001. "Aid and Growth Regressions." *Journal of Development Economics* 64: 547–570.

Hanushek, Eric, and Dongwook Kim. 1995. "Schooling, Labor Force Quality, and Economic Growth." NBER Working Paper 5399. National Bureau of Economic Research, Cambridge, Mass.

International Finance Corporation (IFC). 2001. *OEG Findings* (June). Washington, D.C.: International Finance Corporation.

———. 2002. *Annual Review of IFC's Evaluation Findings FY2001.* Washington, D.C.: International Finance Corporation.

International Monetary Fund (IMF). 1998. *External Evaluation of ESAF: Report by a Group of Independent Experts.* Washington, D.C.: IMF.

International Monetary Fund and World Bank. 2002. *Review of the Poverty Reduction Strategy Paper (PRSP) Approach: Early Experience with Interim PRSPs and Full PRSPs.* Unpublished paper. Washington, D.C..

Jayarajah, Carl, William Branson, and Binayek Sen. 1996. *Social Dimensions of Adjustment: World Bank Experience 1980–93.* Operations Evaluation Study. Washington, D.C.: World Bank.

Johnson, John H., and Sulaiman Wasty. 1993. "Borrower Ownership of Adjustment Programs and the Political Economy of Reform." Discussion Paper No. 199. World Bank, Washington, D.C.

Kapur, Devesh, John P. Lewis, and Richard Webb. 1997. *The World Bank: Its First Half Century.* Volume 1, *History.* Washington, D.C.: Brookings Institution Press.

Killick, Tony. 1999. "Making Adjustment Work for the Poor." Poverty Briefing. Overseas Development Institute, London.

Krueger, Alan, and Mikael Lindahl. 1999. "Education for Growth in Sweden and the World." *Swedish Economic Policy Review* 6(2): 289–339.

Levine, Ross, and David Renelt. 1992. "A Sensitivity Analysis of Cross-Country Growth Regressions." *American Economic Review* 82(4): 942–63.

Maddison, Angus. 1995. *Monitoring the World Economy*. Paris: Organisation for Economic Co-operation and Development.

Narayan, Deepa, and Patti Petesch. 2002. *Voices of the Poor: From Many Lands*. Published for the World Bank. New York: Oxford University Press.

Owens, Trudy, and John Hoddinott. 1998. "Investing in Development or Investing in Relief: Quantifying the Poverty Tradeoffs Using Zimbabwe Household Panel Data." Working paper series No. WPS/99–4. Centre for the Study of African Economies, Zimbabwe.

Pritchett, Lant. 2000. "Understanding Patterns of Economic Growth: Searching for Hills among Plateaus, Mountains and Plains." *World Bank Economic Review* 14(2): 221–50.

Ravallion, Martin. 2001. "Growth, Inequality, and Poverty: Looking Beyond Averages." *World Development* 29(11): 1803–15.

Ravallion, Martin, and Shaohua Chen. 1997. "What Can New Survey Data Tell Us about Recent Changes in Distribution and Poverty?" *World Bank Economic Review* 11(2): 357–82.

Rodrik, Dani. 2001. "Institutions, Integration, and Geography: In Search of the Deep Determinants of Economic Growth." Unpublished paper. Harvard University, Boston, Mass.

Romer, Paul. 1994. "New Goods, Old Theory, and the Welfare Costs of Trade Restrictions." *Journal of Development Economics* 43: 5–38.

Sachs, Jeffrey, and Andrew Warner. 1995. "Economic Reform and the Process of Global Integration." *Brookings Papers on Economic Activity* 0(1): 1–95.

Sahn, David, ed. 1996. *Economic Reform and the Poor in Africa*. Oxford: Clarendon Press.

Sen, Amartya. 1999. *Development as Freedom*. New York: Knopf.

Stern, Nicholas. 2001. *A Strategy for Development*. Washington, D.C.: World Bank.

Stewart, Frances. 1995. *Adjustment and Poverty: Options and Choices*. London: Routledge.

Watkins, Kevin. 1995. *The OXFAM Poverty Report 1995*. Oxford: OXFAM (United Kingdom and Ireland).

West, Gerald T., and Ethel I. Tarazona. 2001. *Investment Insurance and Development Impact: Evaluating MIGA's Experience*. Washington, D.C.: Multilateral Investment Guarantee Agency.

World Bank. Various Years. *Annual Report on Portfolio Performance* (ARPP). Washington, D.C.: World Bank.

——. 1992. *Effective Implementation: Key to Development Impact-Report of the World Bank's Portfolio Management Task Force* (R92–195/2/3). November 3, 1992. Washington, D.C.: World Bank.

——. 1993. *The East Asian Miracle: Economic Growth and Public Policy*. Washington, D.C.: World Bank.

——. 1994a. *Reducing the Debt Burden of Poor Countries: A Framework for Action*. Development in Practice Series. Washington, D.C.: World Bank.

——. 1994b. *Structural and Sectoral Adjustment, World Bank Experience 1980–92*. Operations Evaluation Department. Washington, D.C.: World Bank.

——. 1996a. *Social Dimensions of Adjustment*. Operations Evaluation Department. Washington, D.C.: World Bank.

——. 1996b. *Agricultural Adjustment and Food Policy Reform in Mexico*. Operations Evaluation Department. Washington, D.C.: World Bank.

——. 1997. *China 2020: Development Challenges in the New Century*. Washington, D.C.: World Bank.

——. 1998a. *Assessing Aid: What Works, What Doesn't, and Why*. Washington, D.C.: World Bank.

——. 1998b. *World Development Report 1998/99: Knowledge for Development*. Washington, D.C.: World Bank.

——. 1999a. *Country Assistance Strategies: Retrospective and Implications*. (R99–228), December 7. Washington, D.C.: World Bank.

——. 1999b. *Health Care in Mali: Building on Community Involvement*. Operations Evaluation Department. Washington, D.C.: World Bank.

——. 1999c. *Higher Impact Adjustment Lending (HIAL): Initial Evaluation*. Operations Evaluation Department. Washington, D.C.: World Bank.

——. 1999d. *Investing in Health, Development Effectiveness in the Health, Nutrition, Population Sector*. Operations Evaluation Department. Washington, D.C.: World Bank.

———. 1999e. *The World Bank Grant Program and the Consultative Group on International Agricultural Research (CGIAR).* Operations Evaluation Department. Washington, D.C.: World Bank.

———. 2000a. *An Analysis of Combating Iodine Deficiency: Case Studies of China, Indonesia and Madagascar.* Washington, D.C.: World Bank.

———. 2000b. *Can Africa Claim the 21st Century?* Washington, D.C.: World Bank.

———. 2000c. *Fixing ESW: Where Are We?* (CODE 2000–76), July 11. Washington, D.C.: World Bank.

———. 2000d. *Reforming Public Institutions and Strengthening Governance, A World Bank Strategy.* Washington, D.C.: World Bank.

———. 2000e. *World Development Report 2000/2001: Attacking Poverty.* Washington, D.C.: World Bank.

———. 2001a. "Adjustment from Within: Lessons from the Structural Adjustment Participatory Review Initiative." Prepared for the Second Global SAPRI Forum, July 30–31, Washington, D.C.

———. 2001b. *Adjustment Lending Retrospective: Final Report.* Washington, D.C.: World Bank.

———. 2001c. *Engendering Development through Gender Equality in Rights, Resources, and Voice.* Washington, D.C.: World Bank.

———. 2001d. *Finance for Growth.* Washington, D.C.: World Bank.

———. 2001e. "Fixing ESW: Phase II—Challenges and Net Steps in the ESW Reform Process" (SecM2001–0431), June 28, 2001.

———. 2001f. *Global Economic Prospects 2002: Making Trade Work for the World's Poor.* Washington, D.C.: World Bank.

———. 2001g. *Quality of ESW in FY00–A QAG Assessment* (CODE 2001–0033), April 2. Washington, D.C.: World Bank.

———. 2001h. *World Development Report 2002: Building Institutions for Markets.* Washington, D.C.: World Bank.

———. 2002a. "Estimating the Additional Aid Required to Attain the Millennium Development Goals: The World Bank's Approach, and Comparisons with Other Approaches." Unpublished paper, Human Development Network. Washington, D.C..

———. 2002b. *Globalization, Growth, and Poverty: Building an Inclusive World Economy.* Washington, D.C.: World Bank.

———. 2002c. *Transition: The First Ten Years. Analysis and Lessons for Eastern Europe and the Former Soviet Union.* Washington, D.C.: World Bank.

Acronyms

AERC	African Economic Research Consortium
AIDS	Acquired Immune Deficiency Syndrome
CAE	Country Assistance Evaluations
CAS	Country Assistance Strategy
CDF	Comprehensive Development Framework
CGAP	Consultative Group to Assist the Poor
CGIAR	Consultative Group for International Agricultural Research
CIS	Commonwealth of Independent States
CPIA	Country Policy and Institutional Assessments
DGF	Development Grant Facility
EBRD	European Bank for Reconstruction and Development
ECA	Europe and Central Asia
EIB	European Investment Bank
ERR	Economic rate of return
EU	European Union
GDP	Gross domestic product
GNP	Gross national product
HIAL	Higher Impact Adjustment Lending
HIPC	Heavily Indebted Poor Countries
IBRD	International Bank for Reconstruction and Development
IDA	International Development Association
IFC	International Finance Corporation
IFPRI	International Food Policy Research Institute
LICUS	Low Income Countries under Stress
MDG	Millennium Development Goals
MIGA	Multilateral Investment Guarantee Agency
NGO	Nongovernmental organization
OCP	Onchocerciasis Control Program
ODA	Official Development Assistance
OECD	Organisation for Economic Co-operation and Development
OED	Operations Evaluation Department
OEG	Operations Evaluation Group
OEU	Operations Evaluation Unit
OPCS	Operations Policy and Country Services Unit
PRSP	Poverty Reduction Strategy Paper
QACU	Quality Assurance and Compliance Unit

QAG	Quality Assurance Group
SME	Small and medium enterprises
SSA	Sub-Saharan Africa
SSP	Sector Strategy Paper
STD	Sexually Transmitted Diseases
TB	Tuberculosis
TFP	Total Factor Productivity
UN	United Nations
UNDP	United Nations Development Program
WHO	World Health Organization

Part IV

The Monterrey Consensus

Final Outcome of the United Nations International Conference on Financing for Development, March 2002

United Nations General Assembly

The Monterrey Consensus was adopted by acclamation at the Summit Segment of the United Nations International Conference on Financing for Development on 22 March 2002. This United Nations document[1] is available online at the Monterrey conference web site, **http://www.un.org/esa/ffd/**.

This document is introduced by Mats Karlsson, World Bank vice president for External Affairs and U.N. Affairs.

Introduction

Mats Karlsson

The value of world conferences is often disputed. Both those who are skeptical about the desirability and feasibility of radical change and those who are impatient for it tend to disparage the words and compromises that are the inevitable outcomes of multilateral deliberations. Yet where do the world's people establish the norms and legitimacy to carry on against tough odds? International conferences are not the only resource, but they do play a crucial role.

Be it the Children's Summit in 1990, the Social Summit in 1995, or any other of the major conferences of the 1990s, these events marked a significant coming together around common priorities for an era of new opportunity. The growth of globalization—whereby anyone who wants to control her future must act not only nationally and locally, but also globally—has increased the need for common action and for agendas defining next steps. The idea of global governance has evolved, made progress, and receded, with varying degrees of impact, over the years, but a framework for purposeful political mediation and operational management of our intense global interdependence is only slowly being born. No one can say we are sufficiently meeting these challenges yet.

There is reason, however, to take confidence in the evolving global commitments to practical action. The Millennium Declaration, adopted by heads of state and government from all the world in September 2000 actually managed, against the expectation of many, to state succinctly the values that should bind us and the actions on peace and security, democracy, human rights and the rule of law, sustainable development, poverty eradication, and economic integration that we—the inclusive "we"—should deliver. The declaration showed that it was possible to summarize most of the agreements of the 1990s in clear, meaningful language and to provide a platform for development in the new century.

The Millennium Development Goals (MDGs), which now focus the attention of all development-oriented institutions, derive from that Millennium Summit. And the Monterrey Consensus from the

International Conference on Financing for Development (FfD) in March 2002 spells out further how we can achieve the goals. A global development partnership—in which national responsibility for poverty-reducing strategies is coupled with coherent international action on trade, aid, and in other areas—has been crafted. The proof will lie in the practical action that is to follow and in the real outcomes that we will need to monitor. A joint framework of accountability to rid the world of extreme poverty is in the making.

Conferences can only be assessed properly in light of results. While we do not know how the Monterrey Conference will be assessed in the future, I have confidence that we did make significant progress. Developing countries have demanded a conference of this nature for many years. But it was only after the reforms of the United Nations under Secretary General Kofi Annan and of the World Bank under James Wolfensohn that we had a basis for this coherent step forward.

The wins of Monterrey include:

The Monterrey Consensus. The consensus document is itself a major achievement. It captures in a clear and comprehensive way the financing needs for the MDGs. It spells out the need for good policies, institutions and governance, and addresses the issues of domestic resource mobilization, trade and the private sector, and aid levels and quality—all while maintaining a balance among the mandates of the respective development institutions. No such document has ever been drawn up in the U.N. system, nor had its origin in several years of interinstitutional and intergovernmental work. The document reflects some of the weaknesses of any consensus, but it will provide a better platform than anything we have had before to establish alignment, common ground, and accountability.

The Coherence Imperative. One of the modest but potentially very important wins we hoped for when we set out on the FfD process two years ago was to improve communication between the UN, World Bank, and International Monetary Fund, and to invite greater coherence in what governments say to the respective institutions. In the end, Monterrey was attended by more than 50 heads of state or government, and an equal—and unprecedented—number of finance ministers. In all, more than 300 ministers attended. This attendance demonstrated two things: interest at the highest political level, and a recognition of the need to achieve better coherence in our efforts on poverty and development. Monterrey certainly helped focus our minds; achieving real coherence is another matter.

A Volume Turnaround. Even though the goal of Monterrey was to provide financing for the MDGs, few expected that donors would actually step up to respond to the requests. In the end, pressure built by the conference proved too difficult to resist. By finishing the negotiation of the outcome document in advance, the conference successfully shifted the focus onto what governments would deliver. Both Europe and the United States made hard political commitments to raise levels of aid. If these commitments are delivered upon, the global annual aid volume will rise by some $12 billion or more by 2006—a turnaround after the significant decline in aid levels during the past decade. The increase does not amount to the doubling of aid that the World Bank argues for, but it moves in the right direction. Given the growing consensus that "a dollar in aid lifts private investment by two dollars," the benefits of increasing aid levels become obvious. At the same time, increasing aid is only a good use of money if the results are monitored and continuously improved.

Implementing the Monterrey Consensus means pursuing the new strategic directions that have been laid out in recent years. The partnership approach that James Wolfensohn has taken will be a point of reference for the development community. There is alignment on the poverty objective as expressed in the MDGs and an expectation that donor partners will be accountable. Crucial work includes improving the investment climate, building capacity, delivering on the comprehensive agenda, and ensuring country ownership of the development process.

As development institutions, we must continue showing results, deepen the analysis of our effectiveness, and tie our inputs ever more closely to outcomes. We can make inroads on quality monitoring of bilateral and other aid as well. We can also improve the use of existing aid flows. Refocusing some of the present $53 billion of total aid to benefit those low-income countries with sufficiently good policies would complement the promised increases in aid levels.

The world expects us to "stay engaged," as the Monterrey Consensus phrases the need to improve coherence and governance. The outcome document urges "making the most of existing institutions" while respecting their distinct mandates. Two years of intense collaboration between the United Nations and the World Bank, in particular, to prepare for Monterrey have shown that a new level of interaction is not only possible but present. At both intergovernmental and interinstitutional levels, and in engaging non-state actors, there is much to be done to make the existing system work more efficiently and coherently. There are also essential topics, such as global public goods and innovative financing, that were not addressed at Monterrey but will need multilateral discussion in the near future.

Looking ahead, the unfinished agendas on global issues management will come back in force in the preparation for the World Summit on Sustainable Development in Johannesburg in August-September 2002.

The Monterrey Consensus

United Nations General Assembly

I.   Confronting the challenges of financing for development: a global response

1.   We, the heads of State and Government, gathered in Monterrey, Mexico, on 21 and 22 March 2002, have resolved to address the challenges of financing for development around the world, particularly in developing countries. Our goal is to eradicate poverty, achieve sustained economic growth and promote sustainable development as we advance to a fully inclusive and equitable global economic system.

2.   We note with concern current estimates of dramatic shortfalls in resources required to achieve the internationally agreed development goals, including those contained in the United Nations Millennium Declaration.[2]

3.   Mobilizing and increasing the effective use of financial resources and achieving the national and international economic conditions needed to fulfil internationally agreed development goals, including those contained in the Millennium Declaration, to eliminate poverty, improve social conditions and raise living standards, and protect our environment, will be our first step to ensuring that the twenty-first century becomes the century of development for all.

4.   Achieving the internationally agreed development goals, including those contained in the Millennium Declaration, demands a new partnership between developed and developing countries. We commit ourselves to sound policies, good governance at all levels and the rule of law. We also commit ourselves to mobilizing domestic resources, attracting international flows, promoting international trade as an engine for development, increasing international financial and technical cooperation for development, sustainable debt financing and

external debt relief, and enhancing the coherence and consistency of the international monetary, financial and trading systems.

5.   The terrorist attacks on 11 September 2001 exacerbated the global economic slowdown, further reducing growth rates. It has now become all the more urgent to enhance collaboration among all stakeholders to promote sustained economic growth and to address the long-term challenges of financing for development. Our resolve to act together is stronger than ever.

6.   Each country has primary responsibility for its own economic and social development, and the role of national policies and development strategies cannot be overemphasized. At the same time, domestic economies are now interwoven with the global economic system and, inter alia, the effective use of trade and investment opportunities can help countries to fight poverty. National development efforts need to be supported by an enabling international economic environment. We encourage and support development frameworks initiated at the regional level, such as the New Partnership for Africa's Development and similar efforts in other regions.

7.   Globalization offers opportunities and challenges. The developing countries and countries with economies in transition face special difficulties in responding to those challenges and opportunities. Globalization should be fully inclusive and equitable, and there is a strong need for policies and measures at the national and international levels, formulated and implemented with the full and effective participation of developing countries and countries with economies in transition to help them respond effectively to those challenges and opportunities.

8.   In the increasingly globalizing interdependent world economy, a holistic approach to the interconnected national, international and systemic challenges of financing for development—sustainable, gender-sensitive, people-centred development—in all parts of the globe is essential. Such an approach must open up opportunities for all and help to ensure that resources are created and used effectively and that strong, accountable institutions are established at all levels. To that end, collective and coherent action is needed in each interrelated area of our agenda, involving all stakeholders in active partnership.

9.   Recognizing that peace and development are mutually reinforcing, we are determined to pursue our shared vision for a better future, through our individual efforts combined with vigorous multilateral

action. Upholding the Charter of the United Nations and building upon the values of the Millennium Declaration, we commit ourselves to promoting national and global economic systems based on the principles of justice, equity, democracy, participation, transparency, accountability and inclusion.

II. Leading actions

Mobilizing domestic financial resources for development

10. In our common pursuit of growth, poverty eradication and sustainable development, a critical challenge is to ensure the necessary internal conditions for mobilizing domestic savings, both public and private, sustaining adequate levels of productive investment and increasing human capacity. A crucial task is to enhance the efficacy, coherence and consistency of macroeconomic policies. An enabling domestic environment is vital for mobilizing domestic resources, increasing productivity, reducing capital flight, encouraging the private sector, and attracting and making effective use of international investment and assistance. Efforts to create such an environment should be supported by the international community.

11. Good governance is essential for sustainable development. Sound economic policies, solid democratic institutions responsive to the needs of the people and improved infrastructure are the basis for sustained economic growth, poverty eradication and employment creation. Freedom, peace and security, domestic stability, respect for human rights, including the right to development, and the rule of law, gender equality, market-oriented policies, and an overall commitment to just and democratic societies are also essential and mutually reinforcing.

12. We will pursue appropriate policy and regulatory frameworks at our respective national levels and in a manner consistent with national laws to encourage public and private initiatives, including at the local level, and foster a dynamic and well functioning business sector, while improving income growth and distribution, raising productivity, empowering women and protecting labour rights and the environment. We recognize that the appropriate role of government in market-oriented economies will vary from country to country.

13. Fighting corruption at all levels is a priority. Corruption is a serious barrier to effective resource mobilization and allocation, and diverts

resources away from activities that are vital for poverty eradication and economic and sustainable development.

14. We recognize the need to pursue sound macroeconomic policies aimed at sustaining high rates of economic growth, full employment, poverty eradication, price stability and sustainable fiscal and external balances to ensure that the benefits of growth reach all people, especially the poor. Governments should attach priority to avoiding inflationary distortions and abrupt economic fluctuations that negatively affect income distribution and resource allocation. Along with prudent fiscal and monetary policies, an appropriate exchange rate regime is required.

15. An effective, efficient, transparent and accountable system for mobilizing public resources and managing their use by Governments is essential. We recognize the need to secure fiscal sustainability, along with equitable and efficient tax systems and administration, as well as improvements in public spending that do not crowd out productive private investment. We also recognize the contribution that medium-term fiscal frameworks can make in that respect.

16. Investments in basic economic and social infrastructure, social services and social protection, including education, health, nutrition, shelter and social security programmes, which take special care of children and older persons and are gender sensitive and fully inclusive of the rural sector and all disadvantaged communities, are vital for enabling people, especially people living in poverty, to better adapt to and benefit from changing economic conditions and opportunities. Active labour market policies, including worker training, can help to increase employment and improve working conditions. The coverage and scope of social protection needs to be further strengthened. Economic crises also underscore the importance of effective social safety nets.

17. We recognize the need to strengthen and develop the domestic financial sector, by encouraging the orderly development of capital markets through sound banking systems and other institutional arrangements aimed at addressing development financing needs, including the insurance sector and debt and equity markets, that encourage and channel savings and foster productive investments. That requires a sound system of financial intermediation, transparent regulatory frameworks and effective supervisory mechanisms, supported by a

solid central bank. Guarantee schemes and business development services should be developed for easing the access of small and medium-sized enterprises to local financing.

18. Microfinance and credit for micro-, small and medium-sized enterprises, including in rural areas, particularly for women, as well as national savings schemes, are important for enhancing the social and economic impact of the financial sector. Development banks, commercial and other financial institutions, whether independently or in cooperation, can be effective instruments for facilitating access to finance, including equity financing, for such enterprises, as well as an adequate supply of medium- and long-term credit. In addition, the promotion of private-sector financial innovations and public-private partnerships can also deepen domestic financial markets and further develop the domestic financial sector. The prime objective of pension schemes is social protection, but when those schemes are funded they can also be a source of savings. Bearing in mind economic and social considerations, efforts should be made to incorporate the informal sector into the formal economy, wherever feasible. It is also important to reduce the transfer costs of migrant workers' remittances and create opportunities for development-oriented investments, including housing.

19. It is critical to reinforce national efforts in capacity-building in developing countries and countries with economies in transition in such areas as institutional infrastructure, human resource development, public finance, mortgage finance, financial regulation and supervision, basic education in particular, public administration, social and gender budget policies, early warning and crisis prevention, and debt management. In that regard, particular attention is required to address the special needs of Africa, the least developed countries, small island developing States and landlocked developing countries. We reaffirm our commitment to the Programme of Action for the Least Developed Countries for the Decade 2001–2010,[3] adopted by the Third United Nations Conference on the Least Developed Countries, held in Brussels from 14 to 20 May 2001, and the Global Programme of Action for the Sustainable Development of Small Island Developing States.[4] International support for those efforts, including technical assistance and through United Nations operational activities for development, is indispensable. We encourage South–South cooperation, including through triangular cooperation, to facilitate exchange of views on successful strategies, practices and experience and replication of projects.

*Mobilizing international resources for development: foreign
direct investment and other private flows*

20. Private international capital flows, particularly foreign direct
investment, along with international financial stability, are vital com-
plements to national and international development efforts. Foreign
direct investment contributes toward financing sustained economic
growth over the long term. It is especially important for its potential to
transfer knowledge and technology, create jobs, boost overall productivity, enhance competitiveness and entrepreneurship, and ultimately
eradicate poverty through economic growth and development. A central challenge, therefore, is to create the necessary domestic and international conditions to facilitate direct investment flows, conducive to
achieving national development priorities, to developing countries,
particularly in Africa, least developed countries, small island developing States, and landlocked developing countries, and also to countries
with economies in transition.

21. To attract and enhance inflows of productive capital, countries
need to continue their efforts to achieve a transparent, stable and predictable investment climate, with proper contract enforcement and
respect for property rights, embedded in sound macroeconomic policies
and institutions that allow businesses, both domestic and international,
to operate efficiently and profitably and with maximum development
impact. Special efforts are required in such priority areas as economic
policy and regulatory frameworks for promoting and protecting investments, including the areas of human resource development, avoidance
of double taxation, corporate governance, accounting standards, and
the promotion of a competitive environment. Other mechanisms, such
as public/private partnerships and investment agreements, can be
important. We emphasize the need for strengthened, adequately
resourced technical assistance and productive capacity-building programmes, as requested by recipients.

22. To complement national efforts, there is the need for the relevant
international and regional institutions as well as appropriate institutions in source countries to increase their support for private foreign
investment in infrastructure development and other priority areas,
including projects to bridge the digital divide, in developing countries
and countries with economies in transition. To this end, it is important
to provide export credits, co-financing, venture capital and other lending instruments, risk guarantees, leveraging aid resources, information
on investment opportunities, business development services, forums to

facilitate business contacts and cooperation between enterprises of developed and developing countries, as well as funding for feasibility studies. Inter-enterprise partnership is a powerful means for transfer and dissemination of technology. In this regard, strengthening of the multilateral and regional financial and development institutions is desirable. Additional source country measures should also be devised to encourage and facilitate investment flows to developing countries.

23. While Governments provide the framework for their operation, businesses, for their part, are expected to engage as reliable and consistent partners in the development process. We urge businesses to take into account not only the economic and financial but also the developmental, social, gender and environmental implications of their undertakings. In that spirit, we invite banks and other financial institutions, in developing countries as well as developed countries, to foster innovative developmental financing approaches. We welcome all efforts to encourage good corporate citizenship and note the initiative undertaken in the United Nations to promote global partnerships.

24. We will support new public/private sector financing mechanisms, both debt and equity, for developing countries and countries with economies in transition, to benefit in particular small entrepreneurs and small and medium-size enterprises and infrastructure. Those public/private initiatives could include the development of consultation mechanisms between international and regional financial organizations and national Governments with the private sector in both source and recipient countries as a means of creating business-enabling environments.

25. We underscore the need to sustain sufficient and stable private financial flows to developing countries and countries with economies in transition. It is important to promote measures in source and destination countries to improve transparency and the information about financial flows. Measures that mitigate the impact of excessive volatility of short-term capital flows are important and must be considered. Given each country's varying degree of national capacity, managing national external debt profiles, paying careful attention to currency and liquidity risk, strengthening prudential regulations and supervision of all financial institutions, including highly leveraged institutions, liberalizing capital flows in an orderly and well sequenced process consistent with development objectives, and implementation, on a progressive and voluntary basis, of codes and standards agreed internationally, are also important. We encourage public/private initiatives that enhance the ease of access, accuracy, timeliness and coverage of information on

countries and financial markets, which strengthen capacities for risk assessment. Multilateral financial institutions could provide further assistance for all those purposes.

International trade as an engine for development

26. A universal, rule-based, open, non-discriminatory and equitable multilateral trading system, as well as meaningful trade liberalization, can substantially stimulate development worldwide, benefiting countries at all stages of development. In that regard, we reaffirm our commitment to trade liberalization and to ensure that trade plays its full part in promoting economic growth, employment and development for all. We thus welcome the decisions of the World Trade Organization to place the needs and interests of developing countries at the heart of its work programme, and commit ourselves to their implementation.

27. To benefit fully from trade, which in many cases is the single most important external source of development financing, the establishment or enhancement of appropriate institutions and policies in developing countries, as well as in countries with economies in transition, is needed. Meaningful trade liberalization is an important element in the sustainable development strategy of a country. Increased trade and foreign direct investment could boost economic growth and could be a significant source of employment.

28. We acknowledge the issues of particular concern to developing countries and countries with economies in transition in international trade to enhance their capacity to finance their development, including trade barriers, trade-distorting subsidies and other trade-distorting measures, particularly in sectors of special export interest to developing countries, including agriculture; the abuse of anti-dumping measures; technical barriers and sanitary and phytosanitary measures; trade liberalization in labour intensive manufactures; trade liberalization in agricultural products; trade in services; tariff peaks, high tariffs and tariff escalation, as well as non-tariff barriers; the movement of natural persons; the lack of recognition of intellectual property rights for the protection of traditional knowledge and folklore; the transfer of knowledge and technology; the implementation and interpretation of the Agreement on Trade-Related Aspects of Intellectual Property Rights[5] in a manner supportive of public health; and the need for special and differential treatment provisions for developing countries in trade agreements to be made more precise, effective and operational.

29. To ensure that world trade supports development to the benefit of all countries, we encourage the members of the World Trade Organization to implement the outcome of its Fourth Ministerial Conference, held in Doha, Qatar from 9 to 14 November 2001.

30. We also undertake to facilitate the accession of all developing countries, particularly the least developed countries, as well as countries with economies in transition, that apply for membership of the World Trade Organization.

31. We will implement the commitments made in Doha to address the marginalization of the least developed countries in international trade as well as the work programme adopted to examine issues related to the trade of small economies.

32. We also commit ourselves to enhancing the role of regional and subregional agreements and free trade areas, consistent with the multilateral trading system, in the construction of a better world trading system. We urge international financial institutions, including the regional development banks, to continue to support projects that promote subregional and regional integration among developing countries and countries with economies in transition.

33. We recognize the importance of enhanced and predictable access to all markets for the exports of developing countries, including small island developing States, landlocked and transit developing countries and countries in Africa, as well as countries with economies in transition.

34. We call on developed countries that have not already done so to work towards the objective of duty-free and quota-free access for all least developed countries' exports, as envisaged in the Programme of Action for the Least Developed Countries adopted in Brussels. Consideration of proposals for developing countries to contribute to improved market access for least developed countries would also be helpful.

35. We further recognize the importance for developing countries as well as countries with economies in transition of considering reducing trade barriers among themselves.

36. In cooperation with the interested Governments and their financial institutions and to further support national efforts to benefit from trade opportunities and effectively integrate into the multilateral trading system, we invite multilateral and bilateral financial and development

institutions to expand and coordinate their efforts, with increased resources, for gradually removing supply-side constraints; improve trade infrastructure; diversify export capacity and support an increase in the technological content of exports; strengthen institutional development and enhance overall productivity and competitiveness. To that end, we further invite bilateral donors and the international and regional financial institutions, together with the relevant United Nations agencies, funds and programmes, to reinforce the support for trade-related training, capacity and institution building and trade-supporting services. Special consideration should be given to least developed countries, landlocked developing countries, small island developing States, African development, transit developing countries and countries with economies in transition, including through the Integrated Framework for Trade-Related Technical Assistance to Least Developed Countries and its follow-up, the Joint Integrated Technical Assistance Programme, the World Trade Organization Doha Development Agenda Global Trust Fund, as well as the activities of the International Trade Centre.

37. Multilateral assistance is also needed to mitigate the consequences of depressed export revenues of countries that still depend heavily on commodity exports. Thus, we recognize the recent review of the International Monetary Fund Compensatory Financing Facility and will continue to assess its effectiveness. It is also important to empower developing country commodity producers to insure themselves against risk, including against natural disasters. We further invite bilateral donors and multilateral aid agencies to strengthen their support to export diversification programmes in those countries.

38. In support of the process launched in Doha, immediate attention should go to strengthening and ensuring the meaningful and full participation of developing countries, especially the least developed countries, in multilateral trade negotiations. In particular, developing countries need assistance in order to participate effectively in the World Trade Organization work programme and negotiating process through the enhanced cooperation of all relevant stakeholders, including the United Nations Conference on Trade and Development, the World Trade Organization and the World Bank. To those ends, we underscore the importance of effective, secure and predictable financing of trade-related technical assistance and capacity-building.

*Increasing international financial and technical cooperation
for development*

39. Official development assistance (ODA) plays an essential role as a complement to other sources of financing for development, especially in those countries with the least capacity to attract private direct investment. ODA can help a country to reach adequate levels of domestic resource mobilization over an appropriate time horizon, while human capital, productive and export capacities are enhanced. ODA can be critical for improving the environment for private sector activity and can thus pave the way for robust growth. ODA is also a crucial instrument for supporting education, health, public infrastructure development, agriculture and rural development, and to enhance food security. For many countries in Africa, least developed countries, small island developing States and landlocked developing countries, ODA is still the largest source of external financing and is critical to the achievement of the development goals and targets of the Millennium Declaration and other internationally agreed development targets.

40. Effective partnerships among donors and recipients are based on the recognition of national leadership and ownership of development plans and, within that framework, sound policies and good governance at all levels are necessary to ensure ODA effectiveness. A major priority is to build those development partnerships, particularly in support of the neediest, and to maximize the poverty reduction impact of ODA. The goals, targets and commitments of the Millennium Declaration and other internationally agreed development targets can help countries to set short- and medium-term national priorities as the foundation for building partnerships for external support. In that context, we underline the importance of the United Nations funds, programmes and specialized agencies, and we will strongly support them.

41. We recognize that a substantial increase in ODA and other resources will be required if developing countries are to achieve the internationally agreed development goals and objectives, including those contained in the Millennium Declaration. To build support for ODA, we will cooperate to further improve policies and development strategies, both nationally and internationally, to enhance aid effectiveness.

42. In that context, we urge developed countries that have not done so to make concrete efforts towards the target of 0.7 per cent of gross national product (GNP) as ODA to developing countries and 0.15 to

0.20 per cent of GNP of developed countries to least developed countries, as reconfirmed at the Third United Nations Conference on Least Developed Countries, and we encourage developing countries to build on progress achieved in ensuring that ODA is used effectively to help achieve development goals and targets. We acknowledge the efforts of all donors, commend those donors whose ODA contributions exceed, reach or are increasing towards the targets, and underline the importance of undertaking to examine the means and time frames for achieving the targets and goals.

43. Recipient and donor countries, as well as international institutions, should strive to make ODA more effective. In particular, there is a need for the multilateral and bilateral financial and development institutions to intensify efforts to:

- Harmonize their operational procedures at the highest standard so as to reduce transaction costs and make ODA disbursement and delivery more flexible, taking into account national development needs and objectives under the ownership of the recipient country;

- Support and enhance recent efforts and initiatives, such as untying aid, including the implementation of the Organisation for Economic Co-operation and Development/Development Assistance Committee recommendation on untying aid to the least developed countries, as agreed by the Organisation for Economic Co-operation and Development in May 2001. Further efforts should be made to address burdensome restrictions;

- Enhance the absorptive capacity and financial management of the recipient countries to utilize aid in order to promote the use of the most suitable aid delivery instruments that are responsive to the needs of developing countries and to the need for resource predictability, including budget support mechanisms, where appropriate, and in a fully consultative manner;

- Use development frameworks that are owned and driven by developing countries and that embody poverty reduction strategies, including poverty reduction strategy papers, as vehicles for aid delivery, upon request;

- Enhance recipient countries' input into and ownership of the design, including procurement, of technical assistance programmes; and increase the effective use of local technical assistance resources;

- Promote the use of ODA to leverage additional financing for development, such as foreign investment, trade and domestic resources;

- Strengthen triangular cooperation, including countries with economies in transition, and South–South cooperation, as delivery tools for assistance;

- Improve ODA targeting to the poor, coordination of aid and measurement of results.

We invite donors to take steps to apply the above measures in support of all developing countries, including immediately in support of the comprehensive strategy that is embodied in the New Partnership for Africa's Development and similar efforts in other regions, as well as in support of least developed countries, small island developing States and landlocked developing countries. We acknowledge and appreciate the discussions taking place in other forums on proposals to increase the concessionality of development financing, including greater use of grants.

44. We recognize the value of exploring innovative sources of finance provided that those sources do not unduly burden developing countries. In that regard, we agree to study, in the appropriate forums, the results of the analysis requested from the Secretary-General on possible innovative sources of finance, noting the proposal to use special drawing rights allocations for development purposes. We consider that any assessment of special drawing rights allocations must respect the International Monetary Fund's Articles of Agreement and the established rules of procedure of the Fund, which requires taking into account the global need for liquidity at the international level.

45. Multilateral and regional development banks continue to play a vital role in serving the development needs of developing countries and countries with economies in transition. They should contribute to providing an adequate supply of finance to countries that are challenged by poverty, follow sound economic policies and may lack adequate access to capital markets. They should also mitigate the impact of excessive volatility of financial markets. Strengthened regional development banks and subregional financial institutions add flexible financial support to national and regional development efforts, enhancing ownership and overall efficiency. They also serve as a vital source of knowledge and expertise on economic growth and development for their developing member countries.

46. We will ensure that the long-term resources at the disposal of the international financial system, including regional and subregional institutions and funds, allow them to adequately support sustained economic and social development, technical assistance for capacity-building, and social and environmental protection schemes. We will also continue to enhance their overall lending effectiveness through increased country ownership, operations that raise productivity and yield measurable results in reducing poverty, and closer coordination with donors and the private sector.

External debt

47. Sustainable debt financing is an important element for mobilizing resources for public and private investment. National comprehensive strategies to monitor and manage external liabilities, embedded in the domestic preconditions for debt sustainability, including sound macroeconomic policies and public resource management, are a key element in reducing national vulnerabilities. Debtors and creditors must share the responsibility for preventing and resolving unsustainable debt situations. Technical assistance for external debt management and debt tracking can play an important role and should be strengthened.

48. External debt relief can play a key role in liberating resources that can then be directed towards activities consistent with attaining sustainable growth and development, and therefore, debt relief measures should, where appropriate, be pursued vigorously and expeditiously, including within the Paris and London Clubs and other relevant forums. Noting the importance of re-establishing financial viability for those developing countries facing unsustainable debt burdens, we welcome initiatives that have been undertaken to reduce outstanding indebtedness and invite further national and international measures in that regard, including, as appropriate, debt cancellation and other arrangements.

49. The enhanced Heavily Indebted Poor Countries Initiative provides an opportunity to strengthen the economic prospects and poverty reduction efforts of its beneficiary countries. Speedy, effective and full implementation of the enhanced Initiative, which should be fully financed through additional resources, is critical. Heavily indebted poor countries should take the policy measures necessary to become eligible for the Initiative. Future reviews of debt sustainability should also bear in mind the impact of debt relief on progress towards the

achievement of the development goals contained in the Millennium Declaration. We stress the importance of continued flexibility with regard to the eligibility criteria. Continued efforts are needed to reduce the debt burden of heavily indebted poor countries to sustainable levels. The computational procedures and assumptions underlying debt sustainability analysis need to be kept under review. Debt sustainability analysis at the completion point needs to take into account any worsening global growth prospects and declining terms of trade. Debt relief arrangements should seek to avoid imposing any unfair burdens on other developing countries.

50. We stress the need for the International Monetary Fund and the World Bank to consider any fundamental changes in countries' debt sustainability caused by natural catastrophes, severe terms of trade shocks or conflict, when making policy recommendations, including for debt relief, as appropriate.

51. While recognizing that a flexible mix of instruments is needed to respond appropriately to countries' different economic circumstances and capacities, we emphasize the importance of putting in place a set of clear principles for the management and resolution of financial crises that provide for fair burden-sharing between public and private sectors and between debtors, creditors and investors. We encourage donor countries to take steps to ensure that resources provided for debt relief do not detract from ODA resources intended to be available for developing countries. We also encourage exploring innovative mechanisms to comprehensively address debt problems of developing countries, including middle-income countries and countries with economies in transition.

Addressing systemic issues: enhancing the coherence and consistency of the international monetary, financial and trading systems in support of development

52. In order to complement national development efforts, we recognize the urgent need to enhance coherence, governance, and consistency of the international monetary, financial and trading systems. To contribute to that end, we underline the importance of continuing to improve global economic governance and to strengthen the United Nations leadership role in promoting development. With the same purpose, efforts should be strengthened at the national level to enhance coordination among all relevant ministries and institutions.

Similarly, we should encourage policy and programme coordination of international institutions and coherence at the operational and international levels to meet the Millennium Declaration development goals of sustained economic growth, poverty eradication and sustainable development.

53. Important international efforts are under way to reform the international financial architecture. Those efforts need to be sustained with greater transparency and the effective participation of developing countries and countries with economies in transition. One major objective of the reform is to enhance financing for development and poverty eradication. We also underscore our commitment to sound domestic financial sectors, which make a vital contribution to national development efforts, as an important component of an international financial architecture that is supportive of development.

54. Strong coordination of macroeconomic policies among the leading industrial countries is critical to greater global stability and reduced exchange rate volatility, which are essential to economic growth as well as for enhanced and predictable financial flows to developing countries and countries with economies in transition.

55. The multilateral financial institutions, in particular the International Monetary Fund, need to continue to give high priority to the identification and prevention of potential crises and to strengthening the underpinnings of international financial stability. In that regard, we stress the need for the Fund to further strengthen its surveillance activities of all economies, with particular attention to short-term capital flows and their impact. We encourage the International Monetary Fund to facilitate the timely detection of external vulnerability through well designed surveillance and early warning systems and to coordinate closely with relevant regional institutions or organizations, including the regional commissions.

56. We stress the need for multilateral financial institutions, in providing policy advice and financial support, to work on the basis of sound, nationally owned paths of reform that take into account the needs of the poor and efforts to reduce poverty, and to pay due regard to the special needs and implementing capacities of developing countries and countries with economies in transition, aiming at economic growth and sustainable development. The advice should take into account social costs of adjustment programmes, which should be designed to minimize negative impact on the vulnerable segments of society.

57. It is essential to ensure the effective and equitable participation of developing countries in the formulation of financial standards and codes. It is also essential to ensure implementation, on a voluntary and progressive basis, as a contribution to reducing vulnerability to financial crisis and contagion.

58. Sovereign risk assessments made by the private sector should maximize the use of strict, objective and transparent parameters, which can be facilitated by high-quality data and analysis.

59. Noting the impact of financial crisis or risk of contagion in developing countries and countries with economies in transition, regardless of their size, we underline the need to ensure that the international financial institutions, including the International Monetary Fund, have a suitable array of financial facilities and resources to respond in a timely and appropriate way in accordance with their policies. The International Monetary Fund has a range of instruments available and its current financial position is strong. The contingent credit line is an important signal of the strength of countries' policies and a safeguard against contagion in financial markets. The need for special drawing rights allocations should be kept under review. In that regard, we also underline the need to enhance the stabilizing role of regional and subregional reserve funds, swap arrangements and similar mechanisms that complement the efforts of international financial institutions.

60. To promote fair burden-sharing and minimize moral hazard, we would welcome consideration by all relevant stakeholders of an international debt workout mechanism, in the appropriate forums, that will engage debtors and creditors to come together to restructure unsustainable debts in a timely and efficient manner. Adoption of such a mechanism should not preclude emergency financing in times of crisis.

61. Good governance at all levels is also essential for sustained economic growth, poverty eradication and sustainable development worldwide. To better reflect the growth of interdependence and enhance legitimacy, economic governance needs to develop in two areas: broadening the base for decision-making on issues of development concern and filling organizational gaps. To complement and consolidate advances in those two areas, we must strengthen the United Nations system and other multilateral institutions. We encourage all international organizations to seek to continually improve their operations and interactions.

62. We stress the need to broaden and strengthen the participation of developing countries and countries with economies in transition in international economic decision-making and norm-setting. To those ends, we also welcome further actions to help developing countries and countries with economies in transition to build their capacity to participate effectively in multilateral forums.

63. A first priority is to find pragmatic and innovative ways to further enhance the effective participation of developing countries and countries with economies in transition in international dialogues and decision-making processes. Within the mandates and means of the respective institutions and forums, we encourage the following actions:

- International Monetary Fund and World Bank: to continue to enhance participation of all developing countries and countries with economies in transition in their decision-making, and thereby to strengthen the international dialogue and the work of those institutions as they address the development needs and concerns of these countries;

- World Trade Organization: to ensure that any consultation is representative of its full membership and that participation is based on clear, simple and objective criteria;

- Bank for International Settlements, Basel Committees and Financial Stability Forum: to continue enhancing their outreach and consultation efforts with developing countries and countries with economies in transition at the regional level, and to review their membership, as appropriate, to allow for adequate participation;

- Ad hoc groupings that make policy recommendations with global implications: to continue to improve their outreach to non-member countries, and to enhance collaboration with the multilateral institutions with clearly defined and broad-based intergovernmental mandates.

64. To strengthen the effectiveness of the global economic system's support for development, we encourage the following actions:

- Improve the relationship between the United Nations and the World Trade Organization for development, and strengthen their capacity to provide technical assistance to all countries in need of such assistance;

- Support the International Labour Organization and encourage its ongoing work on the social dimension of globalization;

- Strengthen the coordination of the United Nations system and all other multilateral financial, trade and development institutions to support economic growth, poverty eradication and sustainable development worldwide;

- Mainstream the gender perspective into development policies at all levels and in all sectors;

- Strengthen international tax cooperation, through enhanced dialogue among national tax authorities and greater coordination of the work of the concerned multilateral bodies and relevant regional organizations, giving special attention to the needs of developing countries and countries with economies in transition;

- Promote the role of the regional commissions and the regional development banks in supporting policy dialogue among countries at the regional level on macroeconomic, financial, trade and development issues.

65. We commit ourselves to negotiating and finalizing as soon as possible a United Nations convention against corruption in all its aspects, including the question of repatriation of funds illicitly acquired to countries of origin, and also to promoting stronger cooperation to eliminate money-laundering. We encourage States that have not yet done so to consider signature and ratification of the United Nations Convention against Transnational Organized Crime.[6]

66. We urge as a matter of priority all States that have not yet done so to consider becoming parties to the International Convention for the Suppression of the Financing of Terrorism,[7] and call for increased cooperation with the same objective.

67. We attach priority to reinvigorating the United Nations system as fundamental to the promotion of international cooperation for development and to a global economic system that works for all. We reaffirm our commitment to enabling the General Assembly to play effectively its central role as the chief deliberative, policy-making and representative organ of the United Nations, and to further strengthening the Economic and Social Council to enable it to fulfil the role ascribed to it in the Charter of the United Nations.

III. Staying engaged

68. To build a global alliance for development will require an unremitting effort. We thus commit ourselves to keeping fully engaged, nationally, regionally and internationally, to ensuring proper follow-up to the implementation of agreements and commitments reached at the present Conference, and to continuing to build bridges between development, finance, and trade organizations and initiatives, within the framework of the holistic agenda of the Conference. Greater cooperation among existing institutions is needed, based on a clear understanding and respect for their respective mandates and governance structures.

69. Building on the successful experience of the Conference and the process leading up to it, we shall strengthen and make fuller use of the General Assembly and the Economic and Social Council, as well as the relevant intergovernmental/governing bodies of other institutional stakeholders, for the purposes of conference follow-up and coordination, by substantively connecting, in ascending series, the following elements:

  (a) Interactions between representatives of the Economic and Social Council and the directors of the executive boards of the World Bank and the International Monetary Fund can serve as preliminary exchanges on matters related to follow-up to the Conference and preparations for the annual spring meeting between those institutions. Similar interactions can also be initiated with representatives of the appropriate intergovernmental body of the World Trade Organization;

  (b) We encourage the United Nations, the World Bank and the International Monetary Fund, with the World Trade Organization, to address issues of coherence, coordination and cooperation, as a follow-up to the Conference, at the spring meeting between the Economic and Social Council and the Bretton Woods institutions. The meeting should include an intergovernmental segment to address an agenda agreed to by the participating organizations, as well as a dialogue with civil society and the private sector;

  (c) The current high-level dialogue on strengthening international cooperation for development through partnership, held every two years in the General Assembly, would consider the financing for development-related reports coming from the Economic and Social Council and other bodies, as well as other financing for development-related issues. It would be reconstituted to enable it to become the intergovernmental focal point for the general follow-up to the Conference and related issues. The high-level dialogue would include a policy dialogue, with the participation of the relevant stakeholders, on the implementation of the results of the Conference, including the theme of coherence and consistency of the international monetary, financial and trading systems in support of development;

(d) Appropriate modalities to enable participation in the reconstituted high-level dialogue by all relevant stakeholders, as necessary, will be considered.

70. To support the above elements at the national, regional and international levels, we resolve:

- To continue to improve our domestic policy coherence through the continued engagement of our ministries of development, finance, trade and foreign affairs, as well as our central banks;

- To harness the active support of the regional commissions and the regional development banks;

- To keep the financing for development process on the agenda of the intergovernmental bodies of all main stakeholders, including all United Nations funds, programmes and agencies, including the United Nations Conference on Trade and Development.

71. We recognize the link between financing of development and attaining internationally agreed development goals and objectives, including those contained in the Millennium Declaration, in measuring development progress and helping to guide development priorities. We welcome in that regard the intention of the United Nations to prepare a report annually. We encourage close cooperation between the United Nations, the World Bank, the International Monetary Fund and the World Trade Organization in the preparation of that report. We shall support the United Nations in the implementation of a global information campaign on the internationally agreed development goals and objectives, including those contained in the Millennium Declaration. In that respect, we would like to encourage the active involvement of all relevant stakeholders, including civil society organizations and the private sector.

72. To underpin those efforts, we request the Secretary-General of the United Nations to provide—with collaboration from the secretariats of the major institutional stakeholders concerned, fully utilizing the United Nations System Chief Executives Board for Coordination mechanism—sustained follow-up within the United Nations system to the agreements and commitments reached at the present Conference and to ensure effective secretariat support. That support will build on the innovative and participatory modalities and related coordination arrangements utilized in the preparations of the Conference. The Secretary-General of the United Nations is further requested to submit an annual report on those follow-up efforts.

73. We call for a follow-up international conference to review the implementation of the Monterrey Consensus. The modalities of that conference shall be decided upon not later than 2005.

Notes

1. United Nations document A/AC.257/L13.

2. General Assembly resolution 55/2.

3. United Nations document A/CONF.191/11.

4. *Report of the Global Conference on the Sustainable Development of Small Island Developing States, Bridgetown, Barbados, 25 April–6 May 1994* (United Nations publication, Sales No. E.94.I.18 and corrigenda), chap. I, resolution 1, annex II.

5. *The Results of the Uruguay Round of Multilateral Trade Negotiations: The Legal Texts* (Geneva, GATT secretariat, 1994), annex 1C.

6. General Assembly resolution 55/25.

7. General Assembly resolution 54/109, annex.